HAUNTED ODYSSEY

GHOSTLY TALES OF THE MISSISSIPPI VALLEY

30TH ANNIVERSARY EDITION

JAMES M LONGO

FACTUAL PLANET

ST. LOUIS

Haunted Odyssey originally published in 1986
Factual Planet edition published in 2016

ISBN 978-1-939437-45-7
Cover Design and Photos by Evan Willnow
Copyright © 2016 by Legendary Planet, LLC
Book design by Evan Willnow
Photos by David Becker and as credited
Typeset in Alegreya and Frente H1

Manufactured in the United States of America
Factual Planet is an imprint of
Legendary Planet, LLC
PO Box 440081
Saint Louis, Missouri 63144-0081
LegendaryPlanet.com

TABLE OF CONTENTS

WHY THE BiG MARGIN?

Factual Planet books are designed to promote reader involvement and encourage the reader to get the most from the text.

To that end, all Factual Planet books employ an exceptionally wide margin on the outside edge of each page. Known in book design as a *scholar's margin*, it's useful for readers who want to make notes on a page as they read because it gives them the space to do so. (No more cramming thoughts around the author's name and the page numbers or showers of sticky notes falling out!)

So, please, take your favorite pen or pencil and make use of the space provided for your own comments, thoughts, and questions about the text.

This book is lovingly dedicated to my mother,
who is a true believer—
in me, not the supernatural.

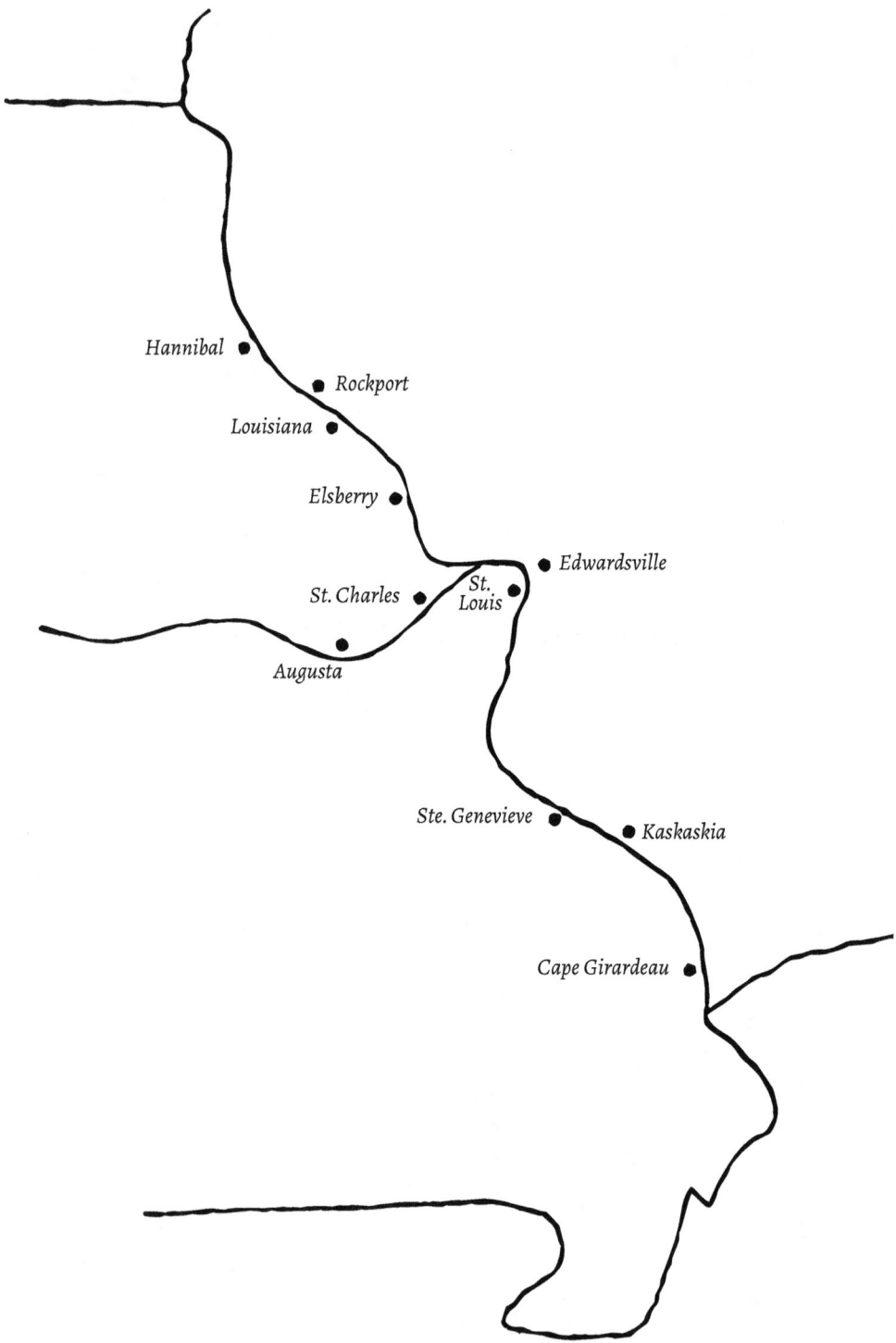

Hannibal

Rockport

Louisiana

Elsberry

Edwardsville

St. Charles   St.
Louis

Augusta

Ste. Genevieve   Kaskaskia

Cape Girardeau

INTRODUCTION TO THE
30TH ANNIVERSARY EDITION

It has been thirty years since I wrote *Haunted Odyssey*. Since that time ghost stories seem to be more popular than ever. It took us three years of searching in Alton, Illinois before we found our first ghost story there. We never gave up. Today that historic river town hosts ghost tours all year round.

Whenever I travel I try to go on as many ghost tours as possible from Edinburgh, Scotland to Prague in the Czech Republic, and from Charleston, South Carolina to Washington, Pennsylvania. Hearing the stories, visiting haunted sites, and meeting the storytellers continues to be fun. But none I have found anywhere match the original stories and storytellers in this book. Many of the *Haunted Odyssey* storytellers remain very much alive, others have crossed over to the other side, and some of the stories continue to this day. Before Bev Elliot died, she and Doug moved to Glen Carbon, Illinois and found an entirely new set of spirited friends in the house they restored there.

My own haunted odyssey continues. I recently returned from Ireland where people talk about ghosts like most people here talk about the weather. When I visited Northern Ireland's amazing Ulster American Folk Park, I was surprised to come across the 1786 ancestral home of the Campbell family. The youngest son in the family immigrated to America, traveled to St. Louis, and became a successful fur trader. His American home, the Campbell House, is now a museum in downtown St. Louis. I often visited there as a child. As I was leaving his original Irish homestead, I asked the docent "Is this house haunted?" She quickly looked around. When she realized no one else was there she said, "Funny you should ask, just last week…"

Simply by asking, I found another story.

And they are everywhere. I have found ghost stories in the rain forests of Costa Rica and the cities of Brazil, from Hampton Court in England to Bran Castle in Romania, and from Harvard University in Massachusetts to the battlefield at Gettysburg. A few years ago President Jimmy Carter and his wife former First Lady Rosalyn Carter shared a story with me about the haunted house where they once lived in their hometown of Plains, Georgia. Seek and you shall find. It never hurts to ask.

I am extremely happy my friend and former student, Patrick Dorsey, author of the bestselling book *Haunted Webster Groves* suggested this thirtieth anniversary was the right time to reissue *Haunted Odyssey*. The stories and storytellers in this book continue to have much to teach us about life, and death. They have taught me many lessons, but two stand out: Nobody likes to be forgotten, and love does not die with physical death.

I hope you enjoy reading these stories as much as I enjoyed collecting them. May all your hauntings be happy ones.

Jim Longo
Washington, Pennsylvania
October, 2016

ACKNOWLEDGEMENTS

Special thanks to all the storytellers, and to...

Jeanne Norberg, David Becker, Mary Costantin, the staff of the Missouri Historical Society, Peg Pizzini, Doris Voerster, Andrea Coe, Liz Hernandez Sanders, Richard O'Brien, Sally Bixby Defty, Sue Ann Wood, Janet Majerus, Jon Morgan, Pat Right, Charles Shipman, Tori Fick, Chris Shumake, Susie Wirthlin, David Borgman and Noel Haydon. Without their support, help and encouragement, this book could never have been completed.

David Becker served as principal photographer for the book with assists from Peg Pizzini and Pat Right.

Special appreciation also to Mrs. Oliver's American Studies classes at University City High School in University City, Missouri, and to the American Youth Foundation campers of Camp Merrowvista in New Hampshire and Camp Miniwanca in Michigan who always wanted "just one more story."

And to Kevin, who I hope is reassured by these stories that "ghosts can be good people, too."

Haunted Odyssey

Ghostly Tales of the Mississippi Valley

by

Jim Longo

Original 1986 cover.

INTRODUCTION

(TO THE 1986 ORIGINAL EDITION)

It was the darkest hiding place I could find.

A long, seemingly empty hallway in a building near my house had become my refuge. In the distance, I could hear them searching for me in all the familiar spots. Their shouts grew closer, then began fading away. My heart was thumping loudly, as only an eight-year-old's heart pounds when he's being hotly pursued in an end-of-summer game of hide-and-seek. For the time being, I was safe—safe enough to take in, slowly, the blackness that touched me on all sides. To my right were the cool shadows that hid me from my seekers. But on my left, I found myself staring, face to face, with the only ghost I had ever met in my entire life.

I was too surprised to be frightened. The figure was about my height, had blurred, milky-white features and a warm, friendly smile. I knew I should be scared, but I wasn't. Then, slowly, very slowly, it reached out, as if to touch me.

That was too much. I tore out of that hallway as fast as my screams and legs could carry me. At home, of course, nobody believed that I'd seen anything real, and maybe I hadn't. But I knew that the feelings of curiosity and of terror I'd experienced were completely real and they have stayed with me a lifetime.

Years passed, but I never really forgot meeting my first, and only, ghost. Then one day I read a magazine article that made fun of the St. Louis region as an area that couldn't even claim a good ghost story. Now, I knew that just wasn't true. I'd heard lots of people tell of having a family ghost or two, but most were pretty shy about sharing their stories.

And that's how this book came to be.

I figured that, in the Mississippi Valley, there had to be all kinds of stories like mine, just waiting to be collected. So, starting in the summer of 1982 in a small river town south of St. Louis and eventually traveling north to Hannibal and south to Cape Girardeau, I visited, listened to, and recorded dozens of storytellers recounting tales of the supernatural. For four years on weekends, vacations, or any time that I could find, I'd grab a tape recorder and a note pad, and search for these storytellers. They turned out to be just about everywhere I traveled, and proved to be just regular folks—a judge in Hannibal, a shop owner in Louisiana, a teacher in Clarksville, a farmer near Elsberry, a blacksmith in Augusta, a college student in Cape Girardeau and many, many more. Housewives, university professors and bus drivers, young and old, black and white, country and city residents, they were a genuine cross-section of the Mississippi Valley's population—with one exception. They, or someone they personally knew and trusted, had had what they believed to be an authentic supernatural experience.

Whenever possible, I've included the names of the storytellers and the actual location of their stories, unless folks requested otherwise. And, at all times, I let them tell their own stories in their own way and in their own words. They, in turn, shared all manner of tales, long and short, funny and sad, scary and not.

Now, are their stories true?

Well, I think that most of the storytellers sincerely believe they are. However, the stories I've collected are not meant to convince the skeptical that ghosts or other forms of the supernatural really exist. They're just meant to be enjoyed.

A word of caution, though, from one of the storytellers. Ezra Tillotson, of Lincoln County, Missouri, shared this bit of wisdom and sage advice: "You've got to be real careful when listening to people because, sometimes, there's enough of the contrary in folks that, if they can wind you a story, they're going to watch your expression real close. And, as long as you're eating, they're gonna keep feeding."

Thanks, Ezra. Good advice. And, to you readers, good reading and *Buon Appetito!*

Jim Longo
Summer, 1986

KASKASKIA,
BY WAY OF STE. GENEVIEVE

The Guibourd-Valle house in Ste. Genevieve.

Where do you begin to look for a good ghost story?

In the Mississippi Valley, the best place to start any search is the river itself. And one of the oldest and most historic river towns close to St. Louis is old Ste. Genevieve. It has a lot of history, and, I hoped, lots of ghost stories, too. So in the early summer of 1982, I found myself driving south along the river, and wondering how I would meet my storytellers and where this haunted odyssey would lead me.

By the time I got to Ste. Genevieve, I still didn't know how or where to begin. I drove slowly around the town square which is dominated by the large Catholic Church and sprinkled about with smaller buildings. When I saw the Tourist Information Center, it seemed as good a place to start as any.

After making my way up the steps of the heavy stone building, and through several minutes of touristy type conversation, I casually asked the local guide, "And, are there a lot of ghost stories in this area?"

Her surprised silence echoed through the room.

Then she said, "I love this kind of thing! Well, let's start with the ghosts in the old Guibourd-Valle House. When you take the tour over there, they don't tell you about them, but they should. It was built in 1785 and is supposedly filled with spirits and poltergeists. The last person to occupy the house was the great-grandson of the last French commandant of Ste. Genevieve. He always claimed he had little imps as friends. He said they used to come into his bedroom and play at the foot of his bed. After he died, his widow didn't want them there. So, one day, she walked straight into the bedroom and asked them all to leave. They did, but they came back. Later, a fine lady from France visited, but didn't stay. She insisted that the sounds from all the previous French occupants were so loud that she had to find lodgings elsewhere!

"And, over at the Bolduc House, two sisters used to live. One of them requested that when she passed away she be buried with her favorite gold medallion. But, after her death, the other woman became greedy. She didn't carry out her sister's wishes. Instead, she kept the gold medal in a bureau that's still found in the Bolduc bedroom. One night, with the house tightly secured, the bureau drawer seemingly opened by itself, and the medal disappeared. To this day, it's never been found.

"Another of the Bolduc House mysteries tells of an old bonnet that still hangs on the back of a chair. When a picture is taken of it, a woman's face supposedly appears under it.

"And behind Market Street is the old Memorial Cemetery. It's the oldest graveyard west of the Mississippi. Local traditions tell that, every Halloween, behind its trees and tombstones, the spirits play a deadly game of hide and seek. Anyone foolish enough to go and watch will be one of the players before Halloween comes around next year."

I asked my storyteller if she knew of anyone in the area who'd had an actual one-to-one encounter with a ghost.

Without hesitation she said, "You need to talk with my cousin in Kaskaskia. Between its Indian curse and its French superstitions, it's just the place you're looking for."

She gave me directions. She even showed me, on my map, the island where her cousin lived, but I still had a hard time finding the tiny spot. I was told that Kaskaskia was the oldest French settlement in the valley still directly populated by its colonial descendants. The French connection, plus an Indian curse, seemed like fertile supernatural hunting grounds. So I headed south with the names of Norman and Naomi Picou taped to my dashboard.

Kaskaskia is in southern Illinois, but the only way to get to the isolated island is through southeastern Missouri. An ancient bridge at St. Mary's, a few miles south of Ste. Genevieve, is the only physical link the lonely island has to the mainland. The bridge itself seemed to sag within an inch or two of the muddy river. And, once over it, I drove for miles on narrow country roads without seeing a soul. Finally, when a few buildings were spotted, I stopped to ask directions. My calls and knocks went unanswered until, finally, at the very last house, a door was slowly opened by an entire family. The woman spoke, but the man and the children just stared. She gave me exact directions to the Picous' house, and then quickly closed the door in my face. I couldn't help wondering if the same reception awaited me at the Picous'.

I needn't have worried. Even uninvited and unannounced, I was welcomed like a long-lost friend. Later, the Picous told me that the small cluster of houses where I'd asked directions was all that remained of the town of Kaskaskia.

Norman Picou turned out to be a deep-voiced, casually dressed gentleman with a firm handshake and sharp, handsome features. He was the local historian, and administrator of and a teacher at the island school. His wife, Naomi, was a friendly, attractive extrovert with a genuine talent for oil painting and storytelling. Together they'd raised six children on the island. When I explained the reason for my visit, they seemed genuinely pleased. They really loved Kaskaskia's local history and weren't afraid to discuss its possible supernatural ramifications.

After they showed me through their modern split-level home, I sat with them on the patio overlooking the ever-present river and listened to Naomi Picou tell of her interest in the supernatural.

"I love the folklore that goes along with the local ghost stories. Why be afraid of it? I never was, and I was brought up on it, listening to my darling grandmother who was a superstitious old French woman. My momma and aunts used to tell the old stories, too. When I was a little girl, I'd sit back in the corner and listen, big eyes and big ears, to the grownups. They'd talk for hours about the old French and Indian superstitions they first heard themselves when they were children.

"But," Naomi continued, "Not all of Kaskaskia's supernatural tales were quite so old. A lot happened right in our own family. My grandmother used to tell a story about her son, who died of diphtheria in 1924. He was just twenty-seven years old, and was so sick on his deathbed that he kept slipping in and out of delirium. He was trying to tell her something, but he never was able to get it out. After he was dead and buried, though, she swore he came back. She was in bed with my grandfather when their dead boy came to visit her. He sat down right on the edge of the bed, then slowly reached over, touched her, and began to tell her something. But Grandpa woke up. He turned over and their son vanished! That was the end of it. He never did come back, and she never found out what it was he'd wanted to tell her.

"A similar experience happened to my mother. When I was only nine years old and my mother was pregnant with my younger sister, my father was killed in a truck-train accident. The night he died, Mom said she knew something was terribly wrong.

"There was an awful storm out, and a bird flew up against the bedroom window with a loud crash. The sound of the fluttering wings and the heavy storm woke her up. It frightened her so bad she couldn't go back to sleep. She just knew it was an omen.

"The next morning, around seven o'clock, they came to tell her that there'd been an accident and my father had been killed. His truck had hit a train as it was going down an embankment. Daddy used to be a fireman on the same train, and he and the engineer knew each other well. The engineer saw Daddy and Daddy saw him. They looked straight at each other but neither could stop, and it just happened.

"Mom didn't know what to do. She had a baby about to be born and a family yet to be raised. But she always swore that after he was dead, Daddy came home, one more time, to tell her goodbye. When he got his last job, you see, he was needing it real bad, 'cause it was the Depression, and he was out of work. He had to take a truck and deliver strawberries before they spoiled. They were perishable and had to be delivered fast, so he didn't get a chance to see Momma again. Later, though I don't know how much longer after the funeral, Mom said she heard his footsteps. He came into the house, across the living room floor and into the bedroom. She said she wasn't asleep, delirious or anything. He just reached over, put his hand on top of her head and tousled her hair a little bit, like he always did. Then he bent over, kissed her on the lips, and that was it. She even called out to my aunt Lucille to check the time, to prove that she was awake. It was a little after midnight. She thought for sure that he'd come back again, but he never did.

"When Momma told us, it just about terrified one of my sisters. She couldn't sleep at night because she was so afraid that Daddy would want to come back to tell her something, too. Not me. I just couldn't stay up for anything. I tried, but just figured that, after visiting Momma, Daddy didn't have anything else he wanted to say to me."

Naomi laughed as she finished a story that she obviously enjoyed telling. But I was curious and asked her if her mother had actually seen her father. With a broad smile, Naomi said,

"No, she didn't see him, but she felt him. She said he was as real as anything, though, because he kissed her full on the lips, and then was gone. She lived to be almost eighty, and you never could convince her that it never happened."

The afternoon was half over by the time that I realized I hadn't heard the story of the Indian curse that had brought me to Kaskaskia. I asked Naomi Picou about it, and her face lit up with enthusiasm.

"I love the story," she quickly volunteered. "I've always been fascinated by it, from the first time I heard it as a little girl growing up on the island.

"Years ago, before the curse, Kaskaskia was a peninsula attached to the mainland. It was a paradise in those days with the town having the largest population in the entire state of Illinois. For a while, it was even the state capital."

As Naomi spoke, I couldn't help thinking of the tiny hamlet I'd visited earlier in the day or of the difficulty I'd had even finding its name on a modern map. I didn't have long to wonder what had happened to Kaskaskia. Norman Picou volunteered the answer. "Today its fifteen thousand acres are being stolen by the river.

"The island's school enrollment is down to nineteen students; ten boys and nine girls in grades one through eight. The old capitol building, streets, levees, stores and churches, the Jesuit seminary, convent, homes, and graveyards have all been washed away. And the population is shrinking, like the island itself."

Naomi spoke up. "I think it's all because of the curse!" With that, she energetically told the story.

"The legend dates from around 1735, when Kaskaskia was a growing, thriving French community and home to a wealthy fur trapper named Bernard. The great joy of his life was his daughter, Maria. But it was hatred, not joy, that eventually took over Bernard's life. It destroyed everything he loved, including Kaskaskia.

Norman and Naomi Picou. They will stay on Kaskaskia.

"When Bernard hired a young Indian brave to work at his trading post, his troubles began. The Indian had been educated by the missionaries. He spoke French and was bright and hardworking. Bernard even became fond of him, until he realized that Maria and the young brave had begun to fall in love. With that, Bernard became enraged. He fired the Indian from his job and spread terrible rumors about him, causing him to be driven out of town. But it was too late. The young man and Maria were deeply in love. He made her a promise to return. Then he vanished.

"Maria was heartbroken, but she waited and hoped. She pretended that nothing was wrong, so as not to arouse her father's suspicions. Several local men even courted her, but none could please her. Then, about a year later, a group of unknown Indians visited Kaskaskia. Disguised among

"...the water silenced the Indian, but not his curse."
Painting by Naomi Picou

them was Maria's love. In great secret, they arranged to rendezvous. They did and quickly fled north.

"When Bernard discovered what had happened, he was filled with hatred and vengeance. With a posse, he raced after the lovers and captured them near Cahokia. Maria begged her father to understand, but he refused. He condemned her lover to die the slow, torturous death of drowning. The young man was silent as he was tied to a log to be set adrift in the Mississippi River—but then he swore his terrible curse.

"Bernard would be dead within the year. And the Indian and Maria would soon be reunited—forever. Kaskaskia would be damned, and all its land cursed. It would never again know peace. The Christian altars of its churches would be destroyed, and its homes abandoned, dilapidated, and destroyed. Even Kaskaskia's dead would be disturbed in their graves and become a breeding ground for fishes of the river.

"Then the water silenced the Indian but not his curse. Within a year, the terrible prophecy began to come true. Maria died of a broken heart. Bernard was killed in a duel. And the river began taking its revenge on Kaskaskia. Time and again, its waters attacked the peninsula until, in 1881, a flood cut it off completely from the mainland, but not before the old cemetery was washed completely away. House after house and street after street were eventually abandoned and then lost to the attacking river.

"And the church," Naomi concluded, "the church was moved again and again, but it didn't do any good. Its altar was finally destroyed in the 1973 flood. The effects of that curse are still felt, even today. Maybe that Indian did have some power, and maybe he didn't. But I believe the legend is true, and the effects of that curse are seen everywhere on what's left of the island."

"The old capitol building, streets, levees, stores and churches, the Jesuit seminary, convent, homes, and graveyards have all been washed away."

"After the 1973 flood, at least a third of the island's population moved away," Norman Picou added. "There are only two teachers left at the local school, and no students enrolled in the kindergarten. Twenty years from now, there probably won't be fifty people left."

As for the Picous? They've vowed to stay. They aren't about to be driven from their island home. They've spent their entire lives with floods, ghost stories, and an Indian curse, and seem quite comfortable and content to remain on Kaskaskia with all three.

THE FAVORITE HAUNTS OF CAPE GIRARDEAU

"...I just accepted the fact that there was a ghost in the house."

"It was the biggest scare I ever had in my entire life. After that night, I just accepted the fact that there was a ghost in the house." Mike Garrity, a student at Cape Girardeau's Southeast Missouri State University, seemed a little surprised by the sureness of his own statement. A good friend I'd taught with suggested Mike and I get together in St. Louis during his summer vacation. And, even though he was still troubled by his experience, he seemed to feel better talking about it.

"Our frat house down at Cape was built by a judge in the last century. At one time, it sat on almost two hundred acres of open land that eventually became the main campus of the university. Local legends even tell that the Missouri state flag was designed there. After the judge's death, the house was willed to the school, and in 1980 it became home to our honorary business fraternity. That's when all the unusual things started happening.

"When I first moved in, I noticed a lot of strange sounds, but I just wrote them off as noises peculiar to any old house. I even made up all kinds of excuses for them, but there was just too much to explain it all away. For instance, in the room used for quiet study, I'd notice that the door would open and close, without a breeze or wind or anything touching it. I'd also hear strange noises in parts of the house where nobody was. It sounded like howling or a person moaning. But no one was around and, again, there was no wind blowing outside. Others heard laughing in the cellar but found nobody there. And one guy, whose room was in the basement, heard a knocking on his door. When he opened it, whoever it was had disappeared. The only way to his room was down a creaky old stairway that, for once, was unusually quiet. Although he didn't see anybody, he figured someone was pranking him. So he hid behind the door and waited. As soon as he heard the knocks again, he quickly swung the door open, but no one was there. The basement was empty, and the stairs were completely quiet.

"Then there was the pacing upstairs in the vacant attic. Everyone heard it. And if anyone found himself alone in the house, it didn't take long to hear 'someone else' walking around. It sounded just like a person going from room to room. One guy even insisted he heard footsteps in a small closet space—where a person couldn't even stand up!

"I'll never forget the first time I realized there might really be a ghost in the house. I'd only been there a few months. One night, when everyone was at a party, I ran back home to get something. The house was pitch black and, without bothering to turn the lights on, I rushed upstairs to my room. While there, I heard footsteps above me in the attic. So I called to see who it was. No answer, but the footsteps continued. With that, I walked up to the attic, turned the lights on, but I didn't find anybody. Then I heard footsteps on the first floor, so I figured someone had come in after me. I went downstairs—and the walking started on the top floor again. Nobody was up there, but I distinctly heard footsteps, and the only way to the third floor was the stairway I'd just used. I really got spooked and decided it was time to leave. As nervous as I was, I could still clearly hear the footsteps, even as I made my quick exit through the front door.

"It seems almost everyone who's lived in the house had a story to tell. One winter, a student went to sleep under two heavy blankets, but woke up in the middle of the night shivering. One blanket was neatly folded up on the couch. But the other was tossed fifteen feet clear across the room. Another student woke to a loud crash. Everything on his desk had been thrown on the floor, as if it had been wiped clean. And still another believed the windows in his room opened themselves. He'd close them before he went to bed, lock his door, and go to sleep. In the morning, his windows would be pushed wide open again, and he'd find himself freezing.

"Finally, like a lot of the guys in the fraternity, I managed to reach a truce with *'whatever'* was in the house. But I still wasn't prepared for what was to come."

Mike swallowed hard, took a deep breath, and continued. "One spring, I found myself again returning to the 'empty' house. It was completely dark inside, with no light at all showing from the outside. I ran into the house and saw something resting in the big overstuffed chair in the living room. As my eyes adjusted to the dark, I recognized it as a human figure. It had no light bouncing off it but looked clearly self-illuminated. I got so many goosebumps that I couldn't even look back. I froze from

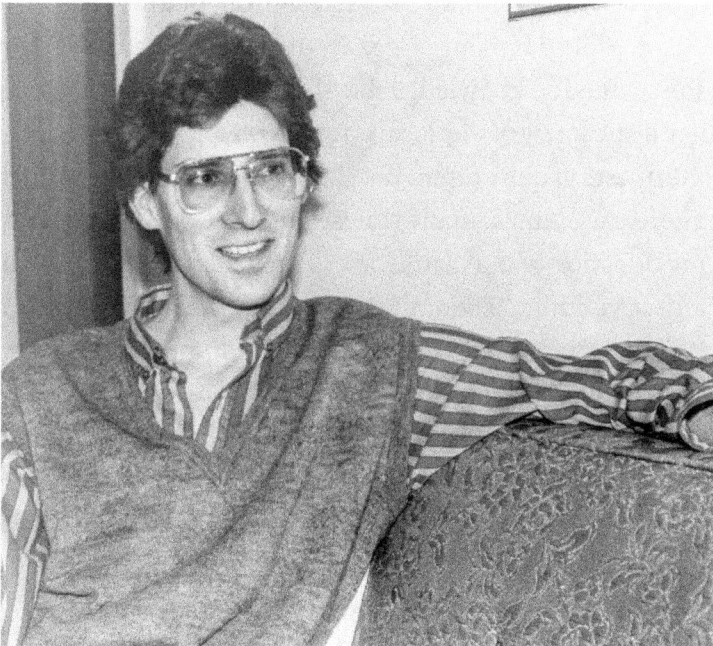

Mike Garrity. *"I know that what they're talking about is all true. I wish I didn't, but I do."*

my neck up. I didn't stop, and it didn't move. It just sat there as tense and as stiff as if it were real flesh and blood. And I just kept walking, too afraid to find out if it wasn't.

"I don't live in the fraternity house anymore," Mike said with obvious relief. "But I still have a lot of friends who do. And, when they talk about the strange things they've heard, and especially when they mention the even stranger things they've seen, I know that what they're talking about is all true. I wish I didn't, but I do."

After hearing Mike's story, I decided to drive down to Cape Girardeau to get a picture of his old fraternity house and look for more stories. I wasn't sure which exit to take into town, but picked one, and promptly got lost in one of the old residential neighborhoods. That's when I accidently found the Cape River Heritage Museum—and the next story.

What better place to ask directions than a local history museum? The woman behind the information desk was businesslike in giving the exact directions needed. In fact, she seemed so knowledgeable that I decided to risk asking her if she knew of any local ghost stories. By now, I'd asked the question quite often. But I knew there was always a risk. There were times, many times, when the only response to my question was a blank look of disbelief. Or a very slight tentative smile. (The smile was usually the worst. It meant I'd been dismissed with equal parts of amusement and sympathy.) This time it was different.

The cool, professional image of my informant melted before my eyes.

"Oh boy, have you come to the right place!" Ann Abbott happily exclaimed as she introduced herself, and added, "This building we're standing in is haunted!"

Even before I could ask her about the museum, Ann enthusiastically began asking me questions about ghosts and the stories I'd already collected. Only when all her questions were answered, did she tell about the ghost at the Cape River Heritage Museum.

"This building was built around the turn of the century, but its foundations, and the original cellar, are antebellum. During the Civil War, it was used as a prison where the inmates were chained to its massive stone walls. Later, it was used as City Hall, the police station, the jail, a fire house, and, finally, it became the museum. It also serves as the temporary home of the community theater company, and that's how I first came here.

"We were using part of the museum to stage our plays until we had a permanent theater of our own. I'd heard stories from several people who'd worked here about strange footsteps, especially footsteps climbing a staircase that wasn't there! Later, we found out that an old staircase had once actually been in the spot where the noises had been heard, but it had been removed years before.

"Well, I heard those sounds, too, but ignored them. Until, one night, I was sitting in this office by myself, and heard someone open and close the back door. I thought it was one of the kids coming to work. I waited, but no one came in. So I went and looked. I just figured, 'Okay that's probably understandable, there's a logical reason'—but I sure couldn't figure it out. Another day, one of the volunteers and I were in the office when someone knocked on the wall. It was a very clear knock, so we figured that one of the other workers was signaling us to come to the back room. We both went back but, again, nobody was there. Nobody. The doors were locked, yet we had both clearly heard it. So, we just went back to work, and it didn't happen again until two days later. Then, when another woman and myself were working, we heard different, strange sounds all night. We were kept busy making excuses for them. That's when the smell came.

"All of a sudden, the very strong smell of turpentine came into the building. We figured that someone had turned over a can. But, when we went through the place, there was no one in the museum, no one in the theater and no overturned turpentine. In fact, the smell was only in the front office. It was overpowering, so strong, you could barely breathe. So we sat down and began talking and arguing, back and forth. Somehow, I figured my friend had done this as some kind of joke. Then the most awful odor that I have ever smelled in my life overcame me. It was indescribable. Horrible. *Horrible.* And I became ill, throwing-up ill. I ran, gagging, into the bathroom. But my friend thought I was putting her on, because she sat just a few inches from me and smelled nothing. I finally told her that the smell was the worst I'd ever experienced. But she still didn't smell anything. Then, a few seconds later, she, too, was assaulted by it. But it was only in the small area of the office. It didn't permeate the halls, bathroom, theater, or museum—just one small radius in the front office, right where we'd been sitting.

"We've tried and tried to find logical reasons or excuses for the sounds and smells, but now we feel we probably just share the quarters with 'past residents'. We can't seem to come up with any other excuses, so maybe we have ourselves a theater ghost. Others insist, though, that it was in the building even before we arrived. Some say we should get an exorcist or 'ghost buster' in and do something about it. And others feel we should just ask it what it wants, because there are always ways to get rid of it. But we don't want to get rid of it. If we've really got it, we want to keep it." Ann smiled as if talking about an old friend.

"All my life, I've been fascinated with the supernatural, and especially ghost stories. I think I spent half of my childhood searching for every ghost story and haunted house I could find in Cape Girardeau."

Ann Abbott

"It somehow seems appropriate that, with its rich supernatural heritage, Cape Girardeau's local history museum should have its own ghost."

It didn't take long to convince Ann to take me on a supernatural tour of the best haunts in her home town. After a quick visit to get a picture of Mike Garrity's fraternity house, I picked up Ann and headed downtown towards the river. Our first stop was a typical city playground where Ann told me she heard her first ghost story.

"It was about a lost child who'd wandered off from a large white mansion that sat overlooking the river on one side, and the playground on the other. Even years ago it was an old story, and told of how the little boy fell in the nearby pond and drowned. He must have called for help, but no one heard him. After the drowning, though, people started hearing the pitiful sound of a crying child, coming from the pond. His family moved away, the pond was drained and filled in, but the crying continued. To this day, folks still claim they hear him.

"I'll never forget the first time I heard it as a child. It was terrifying, but it was sad, too. It was the saddest cry I ever heard in my entire life. I've heard it again, since then, and it's always the same. Now maybe it was the wind, or somebody's idea of a terrible joke, but I don't think so. After that I always knew what people meant when they said that something was haunting, because I'll remember that sound forever. And even today, the neighborhood kids still tell the story. You never see them walk by that hillside. They run past it, as fast as I did when I was their age."

Lorimier Cemetery is the oldest graveyard in Cape Girardeau, and was my next stop with Ann. Weathered tombstones tilt at every possible angle on a hilltop overlooking the Mississippi River. From this vantage point, Ann pointed out a long, low, abandoned house and identified it from her childhood memories, as "the murder house." Next to it was a small red brick building that, Ann told me, was where local legends claim a man was stabbed, repeatedly, and hung up in the rafters to bleed to death.

"When I was growing up, you could see a stain on the floor we all thought was blood. But the part that really scared us was that, if you listened carefully, you could hear 'blood' dripping at night! Now when I got a little older, I got up the nerve to check the place out. I went in to figure out where the sound came from, but there was no sink, no faucet or water of any kind inside. After I left, I figured the dripping must have just been my overactive imagination. But I listened from the outside and, sure enough, I could clearly hear the drip, drip, dripping." Ann laughed. "Some parts of childhood just die harder than others. For me, it must be my hearing!"

Ann also told of the Indian legend of a large, man-eating, grey wolf that supposedly haunted the rocky cape from which the town had drawn its name, and about a local house that had been part of the Underground Railroad. At the house, slave hunters had caught a glimpse of a runaway slave in an upstairs bedroom mirror. The slave had been caught and killed during his escape attempt, and no mirror in that same bedroom had ever remained unbroken.

Ann recalled story after story she'd heard about the supernatural while she was growing up in Cape Girardeau. For every period of the town's rich history, she had a story to tell.

But, Ann admitted, when she was a teenager, her curiosity about such things had come to a screaming halt. By that time, she had gotten used to the 'typical' ghost story and was looking for the unusual. She found it, out on the Gordonville Road, southwest of Cape Girardeau. (That old highway is rumored to be the most haunted in Missouri, with dozens of ghost stories that date back to Indian and pioneer days.) So, naturally, that was our next stop. The hilly country road looked just as it had when, years before, Ann and a friend decided to investigate. Ann remembered feeling sure their adventure would produce a ghostly encounter. All they wondered was which of the many Gordonville ghosts they'd come across.

Ann said she had been hoping to hear one of Mad Lucy's screams. She explained:

"Mad Lucy was a young pioneer woman whose family once lived along the road. Some believed the isolation, loneliness, and hardships of the frontier drove her insane. Others claimed an unhappy love affair caused her to lose her mind. And a few even whispered that strange, unearthly spirits pushed her over the edge. Regardless of the reason, she went crazy and was locked up in the family homestead. Her shrill screams and hysterical crying became a sadly familiar sound to the people who passed on the Gordonville Road. It wasn't until people in the vicinity investigated the sudden absence of Mad Lucy's family that it was found that the farm was abandoned. There was no trace of its owners. They'd just disappeared. But Mad Lucy's unearthly screams didn't. They could still be heard, and continue to frighten travelers, right up to the present."

Ann said that on that day long ago she could hardly wait to hear Mad Lucy. Her friend was hoping to see one of the phantom ghost lanterns she'd heard about.

"Those stories started a century before, when two women were trying to get home from a social before it was too dark. A fog rose up that made the dangerous road even more deadly than usual. On one especially sharp curve, the horses suddenly became spooked. What frightened them? Nobody knows. Maybe it was a scream from Mad Lucy. Anyway, the horses reared up and caused the carriage to overturn. One of the women was crushed under the vehicle, impaled on a broken wheel. The other was badly injured but she tried desperately to flag down help by waving her lantern through the thickening fog. But, in the morning, both women were found dead. After that, people claimed

The Gordonville road where Mad Lucy screams.

that just at sunset, when the evening mists rose, they could see a phantom light waving and dancing in the dark. Supposedly, it was the dead lady's ghost, waving her lantern to warn others of the dangerous curve that killed her and her friend."

Ann admitted, "We didn't care which of the ghosts we found, but we both agreed who we didn't want to find. To us, it was all fun and games, except for one tale we'd heard about a headless ghost. Nobody knew how he'd lost his head. And we didn't care. That story, we could have done without.

"Once we were there, we waited and waited for the sound of Mad Lucy's screams or the sight of a dancing lantern. But they never came. The wind started kicking up, and it got darker and darker, and still no scream, no strange light. The later it got, the less patient we were—and the more we started talking nervously about the headless man. We decided to start walking home.

"When we got to the crossroad near Mount Tabor Park, we saw him. He was at the crest of the hill, just as the last of the sun was vanishing. And he walked very slowly, right in our direction. At first, we were too stunned to think or scream or move. It was like our air supply had vanished, and all the sounds around us just stopped.

"He was headless. Well, not quite. In the crook of his arm he was cradling a head. Then—POOF! He just vanished, disappeared, right in front of us. I don't remember how we got home, but we were still screaming when we got there."

Ann finished her story:

"After that, ghost stories lost their charm for a long, long time. I didn't even like to talk about them. But recently, I've started enjoying them again. And, as for the strange things at the Cape River Heritage Museum, that doesn't bother me at all. In fact, it somehow seems appropriate that, with its rich supernatural heritage, Cape Girardeau's local history museum should have its own ghost."

EDWARDSVILLE`S
THREE MILE HOUSE

The Three Mile House shortly before it burned.

*I*t was one of those days.

Three different interviews had fallen through, and it wasn't even noon. Plan B was to try to find a haunted restaurant that I'd heard about near Edwardsville, Illinois, but, as luck would have it, the restaurant had recently gone out of business. I knew the names of its former owners, but they'd moved away without leaving a forwarding address. And there was no new listing for them in any of the local telephone directories. The old place was for sale, but the town's real estate agent wouldn't give out any information about the owners.

With nothing else to go on, and nothing else to do on a warm summer day, I headed east toward Edwardsville. Two of my former students were home from college and came along to keep me "honest." They were total skeptics about "ghosts, hauntings and all other such silly superstitions", which didn't bother me in the least. In fact, I was glad to have their company.

We crossed the Mississippi and drove into the flat farmlands of Illinois. Outside of Edwardsville, we stopped and asked directions from gas station to gas station as we slowly made our way out Highway 159 toward the old Three Mile House Restaurant, just northeast of Edwardsville.

And we found it. Sitting all by itself on a lonely stretch of country road, the closed restaurant looked just like the classic Hollywood haunted house. Its three stories were dark, gloomy, and ugly. The windows were shuttered, and all the doors were tightly nailed shut. Without a hint of skepticism or college sophistication, one of my passengers muttered under her breath, "If this place isn't haunted, it should be."

After exploring the grounds and inspecting the building from the outside, we made our way to the nearest neighbors. All they could tell us was that the moving van of the previous owners, the Elliots, had turned right on the intersecting county road we could see on the far horizon.

It wasn't much, but it was all we had. So we drove on, looking for the Elliots—and their story. After driving for some time, we stopped again to ask a man cutting his grass whether he had ever heard of the Elliots. He turned off his mower and asked us why we wanted to know. I explained we were collecting ghost stories and hoped the Elliots might be willing to share their experiences in the Three Mile House. Very carefully, he looked the three of us over. Then he said, "They might."

That's when I realized that we were talking with Mr. Elliot. "What do you want to know?" Doug Elliot slowly asked, after introducing himself. "Everything," we told him. But Doug shook his head, *no*. "I'll tell you some of the story, but not everything." Just then, Doug's wife, Bev, came out on the back porch and introduced herself. After she'd offered us something cool to drink, and encouraged us to get out of the hot summer sun, we all sat down under a big shade tree to talk of the Three Mile House. Like Doug, Bev was friendly, but reluctant to say too much. At last, though, they agreed to tell their story.

Doug began. "The first time we saw the Three Mile House was several years ago. We had taken a ride in the country and were lost, when we came across this big, old, rundown, empty hotel. I fell in love with it immediately, but Bev didn't. I'd always wanted to renovate an old building and maybe turn it into a restaurant."

"But," Bev interrupted, "I thought it would be just be too much work. We talked about it for a while, but then drove on, and just forgot about it."

Doug continued, "Four years later, a real estate man neither of us had ever seen before knocked at our door. Out of the blue, he offered to buy our house. We really were caught by surprise because we had no plans to move. But he made a real attractive offer and said that he'd even help us find a new home. After talking it over with our two young daughters, we decided to sell. The first time we went looking for a new house, though, he drove us out a country road that looked vaguely familiar. We didn't think much about it—until he pulled up to the still-empty Three Mile House."

"We were dumbfounded when we saw it again," Bev said. "He told us the house was meant for us. It had a lot of history, too. At different times, it had been a stage coach stop, a station on the Underground Railroad, an old post office, a tavern, a restaurant, and a country inn. Abraham Lincoln had supposedly stayed there in the 1850s. Then he added, with a laugh, 'It's even supposed to have a ghost or two in the attic.'

"We didn't know what to say we were so caught by surprise. It had been twelve years since anybody had lived there, and it was practically a ruin. But now Doug and I both felt drawn to it. Within a short while, we decided to make it our new home and eventually open it up as a restaurant. At that time, we had no idea how the Three Mile House, and its ghosts, would change our lives."

"Moving day was unbelievably hectic. At times, we were really excited, but when we looked at the amount of work that had to be done, it was hard not to be discouraged."

"Lori, our oldest daughter, was fifteen at the time, and the first to encounter anything unusual about the house. Carrying a bulky box into the basement, she suddenly was hit in the leg by a large brick that seemed to fly through the air by itself. Putting the box down, she set out her own ground rules. She said she'd heard that the house was haunted, but she didn't care. 'They' would have to put up with her, just like she was going to have to put up with 'them'. This house belonged to the Elliots now, and the Elliots were there to stay! After her little speech, there was no more trouble that day.

"The next year was almost constant backbreaking, hard work, reinforcing floors, putting in modern plumbing, cleaning and fixing and repairing everything from top to bottom. Hardly a day passed that didn't have new surprises. Tunnels were found in the cellar that extended in every direction and bricked up secret rooms were found underneath the backyard. We figured they were probably hiding places for slaves in the Underground Railroad—but we didn't know what to think about the sparks of light or energy that darted around every night inside or outside, in any kind of weather. They weren't lightning bugs, and electricians couldn't explain them either.

"And Lynn, our thirteen-year-old daughter, swore that darting shadows were always chasing about her room. We didn't know what they were, but Lori and some of her friends thought they knew. They decided to have a séance one night in the attic. With a Ouija board and candles, they went up to the third floor to check out their suspicion. Loud bangings began almost immediately, and then wouldn't stop. They ran screaming downstairs, terrified that the floor would cave in. After that night, and the brick thrown at her on moving day, Lori never doubted that the house was really haunted.

"The darting shadows, the sparks of light, even the loud banging were, by then, regular events usually centered in the basement and attic. We all got used to it, but our family pets didn't. "It was in October of 1977 that I first became really scared by something in the house," Doug said. "Bev was asleep when I woke up at two in the morning. Our room was lit by a full moon, but I knew we weren't alone.

At the foot of the bed, the light was obscured by the massive figure of a three hundred pound black man, well over six feet tall. He was wearing grey, Levi's-type work pants and a grey work shirt that made him look like the Incredible Hulk. I was so terrified to see a burglar standing over my bed, that I felt like my ribcage had collapsed. I couldn't yell or even breathe, and just waited for the blow to fall.

But it never did. Finally he turned around and left the room. Slowly, I got out of bed and climbed out the bedroom window onto the kitchen roof. I nearly jumped, too—I was so shaken—even though it was thirteen feet off the ground! Then I got control over myself and went back in the room to get my gun. I searched the whole house, terrified of what I might find. But all the doors and windows were locked from the inside and nobody was there. Finally, I fell asleep in a cold sweat with the gun in my lap."

"When I woke him in the morning, he was still shaking with fear," Bev said. "He told me about the prowler and we talked a long time about whether or not to tell the girls. But when we finally did tell them, Lori said it was just 'Herman'. He was a harmless black ghost she saw all the time. She said he was probably just trying to communicate with us. Doug told her, 'He picked a hell of a way to communicate. Next time, tell him to use the phone!'

"Lori said she would talk with him about it. Later, when Doug asked her if she had spoken to Herman, Lori laughed. Not only had she spoken to him, but now, whenever he saw Doug, he fled in fear."

"We didn't know what to think anymore," Doug said. "The girls had quickly come to accept the possibility that the house was haunted, but we were both still skeptical and now a little scared!"

"I was still working a full-time job on the railroad and then coming home each night trying to get the house in shape. (Later, the house was listed on the National Register of Historic Places, but that was still an exhausting way off.) Getting up in the morning had become a real struggle. With so much work to do, there was little time to think, talk, or even sleep. One day, my boss told me that if I was late one more time, I'd be fired. I was so depressed and upset that I fell asleep that night with my clothes on before I had set the alarm to wake me up.

"Early the next morning, I heard the sweetest voice I've ever heard say, 'Wake up, Doug, get up!' I thought at first it was Bev, but the voice was different. It sounded like a little girl, beautiful and almost angelic. When I looked over at Bev, she was sound asleep. I realized the time and quickly jumped up and rushed to work. It was the first time in weeks that I hadn't been late. In fact, I was early. The other workers even sent up a cheer. The next morning, the voice woke me up again. When I started to fall back to sleep. I was tugged and rocked until I got up. I was even earlier that morning.

"I named her Sarah, and she continued to wake me up as long as we lived in the house. I never mentioned her to anybody else, because Bev never seemed to hear her, and I wasn't sure what my daughters would think. But, like them, I now believed that we shared our house with ghosts.

"After about a year, I asked Sarah to 'materialize' for me. I had really fallen in love with her voice and wondered what she looked like. But she didn't appear. Instead, I heard Lynn's door slam so I went to her room. When I asked her about Sarah she said, quite matter-of-factly, that she'd never seen Sarah either, but had been awakened by her several times. Lynn described the beautiful, young voice and said that whenever Sarah woke her up, she felt good all day.

"Much later, when psychics from all over the world came to visit the Three Mile House, they often told of seeing a pretty blonde-haired girl of about nine who, it turned out, had died many years before in the house. Her real name was Celia, and her job at the inn when she was alive had been to wake up the lodgers!"

In the spring of 1976, local newspapers announced that the landmark would soon be opened as a restaurant. But as the day grew closer, Bev started worrying that the "ghosts" might scare away the customers. On opening night, her worst suspicions seemed confirmed.

"The first night, just before the customers were admitted, the heavy chairs started sliding away from the tables and began rocking back and forth. Then the dishes began moving about in the china cabinets. But, when the first guest arrived, all the loud activity in the main dining room stopped. Everything became quiet, and I was tremendously relieved. But not for long.

"At first, the ghosts were only active around the family; later they performed for the restaurant workers. Within a year, they were 'teasing' the customers, too. One well-dressed woman from St. Louis complained about the noisy china in the cabinet. I told her that sometimes when trains went by, the china rattled—even though we were miles from the nearest track. The woman said, 'No, they didn't rattle. They moved! Also, the waitresses are having trouble because the drinks keep tipping over by themselves!' All I could say was 'It's been an active night.' On other occasions, the tables moved away from the diners. One set of customers complained they had moved their chairs three times, trying to catch up with their food!

"After we had been open a while, newspapers in the area began giving us very good restaurant reviews. Eventually, we even won several awards. But in the beginning, when papers came to review the food, they often ended up writing about the ghosts, too. In October of 1979, the Alton *Telegraph* wrote an article they called 'Spirited Restaurant Has One Non-Paying Guest'. And another reporter during a visit coolly mentioned that she'd heard the Three Mile House was haunted, quickly adding that she didn't believe in such nonsense. Just then, a large ornamental clock, that hadn't worked for years, suddenly bonged. The newspaper woman said, 'I thought when I came in that the hands of that clock weren't moving.'

" 'They weren't,' I told her. 'It's still broken.' She demanded to know what made it bong. But all I could think to say was 'What do you think?' She titled her story, 'Good Food and Spirits, Too.'

"The newspaper stories helped business," Bev continued, "and even put us in contact with psychics who tried to unravel some of the mysteries of the house. One of them was Robert Mitchum's son, Chris. He came all the way from California to investigate Three Mile House. His theories were typical of many psychics who, for the next four-and-a-half years, told and retold stories that were remarkably similar.

"Most believed that twelve-and-a-half ghosts lived in the house! The 'half' spirit was a woman who was visible only from the waist up. She had long beautiful blonde hair and appeared to be in a panic. They also told us that the large black man that Doug had seen earlier, and that Lori called Herman, was really named Tom. He was the unofficial leader of all the other spirits. Tom had been a runaway slave, brutally murdered on the Underground Railroad. He was buried in a tunnel underneath the house, and his spirit wasn't at rest because he'd been deeply religious and had never received a Christian burial. Doug was touched by the story and actually looked for the grave. But there were so many tunnels, he was never able to find the right one. That was in 1980 and, by that time, almost anything about our ghosts was big news. The *Edwardsville Intelligencer* even ran story about Doug's search and headlined it, 'Man Searches for Body So Spirit Can Rest.'

"...Almost anything about our ghost was big news."

"The psychics told other stories too. Another 'resident' was a lady in black who'd caught her fiancé with another woman. She shot them both, and then hung herself in the attic. In the cellar was the ghost of a Civil War army deserter who had been hung on one of the beams. On the beam was written in plaster, '...died here ... 18...' There was also the spirit of an Irishman in a brown derby down there. But the worst thing they told us was that our cellar was the setting of a real horror story.

"When the house was a hotel for travelers, many who stopped never left alive. They were murdered and dropped through a trap door by the hotel barber who regularly slit his customers' throats for their money. He dropped them through the floor, and then buried them in the old Underground Railroad tunnels. One man, not quite dead when his throat was slit, was knocked out by the fall and buried alive. He still haunts the house, too. The tunnels were also supposedly the grave for dozens of women and children slaves, lured there in search of freedom but quickly murdered, while their menfolk were then sold back into slavery.

"But not all the ghosts had such sad or tragic lives. Doug's wakeup caller, Sarah, was often described by the psychics as generally happy in the house with her adopted family.

"So many different psychics, from all over the world, told us the same stories, that it was hard not to believe them. They even told me that if I'd give orders to the ghosts, they'd obey me. To test their theory, one evening, when the noises in the attic were especially loud, I told all the spirits on the third floor to go to the basement. Within a few seconds, a tremendous racket exploded from the cellar as restaurant workers, who had been meeting there, bolted up the stairs and erupted out into the hallway. They said the basement had filled up with 'spooky' shadows, sounds, and confusion. They'd exited from there in record time." Bev laughed out loud as she remembered the commotion and excitement of that night.

And Doug laughed, too, as he reminisced. "One of the most playful spirits turned out to be Tom, the large black ghost. He gradually warmed up to me and even used to follow me to work on the railroad. Tools would appear and disappear regularly, and the bell on the train would seem to ring by itself on days when I felt Tom was there. He loved to play with the water at the restaurant, too, leaving faucets running and flooding the bathrooms and kitchen. That was really irritating, because water was so expensive and had to be trucked in daily. Bev exploded one morning and told Tom to 'play somewhere else!'

"For the next few days, he wasn't heard from, until one of the waitresses came in very upset and said that she couldn't work afternoons any longer. Bev asked the reason and was told, 'He's found a new toy. All afternoon Tom's been amusing himself turning the large, iron-plated antique coffee grinder, and the clanking noise is driving me crazy.'

The restaurant workers, like the family, had simply come to accept the fact that the Three Mile House was more than a little haunted.

Bev remembered a conversation with one of her straight-laced neighbors who called sounding really upset. '

" 'I've got one of your people here,' she said.

" 'You mean, one of my daughters?'

" 'No! I mean the *other* kind of people!'

" 'O-o-oh. One of *those* kind of people. Well, have they hurt you? Have they done anything wrong?'

" 'Well, no!'

" 'Then how do you know they're there?'

" 'Well, she's wearing perfume and I can smell her when she comes into the room!'

"That's when I realized that the perfume lady hadn't been home the past several days," Bev said. "Although I still wasn't used to giving orders to the spirits, I told the neighbor to tell 'her' that Mrs. Elliot said to come right home. That was the last I heard from the neighbor, but I did begin to smell perfume around the house again."

Doug and Bev Elliots' stories about their experiences in the Three Mile House were filled with such genuine affection and good humor that I wanted to ask them why they had ever moved. But before I could ask, my "skeptical" former students began enthusiastically asking questions about how the Elliots' daughters related to the family ghosts.

The Elliots explained that, maybe because the girls had been so quick to accept the ghosts, there seemed to be a special bond between them. Lynn said she had reluctantly shooed them out of her room on prom night because she was afraid she would step on them. They seemed so excited and nervous about the evening that they were acting more like little brothers and sisters than ghosts! And later, when Lynn had really painful problems with her legs, she said that Tom would come and sit with her. She said she always felt such good strength, sympathy, and support when he was there silently communicating with her.

"Later," Doug said, "when Lori traveled to college in Utah, she believed that one of the spirits had even come along with her. The trip to school had been during a terrible blizzard and many of the cars on the road had stalled or even crashed, killing several people. Lori had felt almost serenely safe during the journey but, when she arrived at school, she began noticing some of the regular ghostly patterns that she had known so well at home. She later came to feel that the ghost had come along to protect her. Having a ghost at school didn't bother her, but apparently he moved out of Lori's apartment into a neighbor's, who wasn't too thrilled." Bev recalled, "I received a long distance phone call from Lori's next door neighbor who complained that the spirit kept turning his stereo rock music off, was continually playing with the typewriter and would whistle in his face. 'So that's where he's been,' I said. 'Well, be firm and tell him to stay in Lori's room where he belongs.' Later, after consulting with a psychic to be sure he would be safe and not get lost, I had Lori send the spirit back. When I heard the typewriter typing by itself, I was relieved to know that he was safely home. Even then, I still couldn't believe that I was really talking to ghosts, and accepting them like members of the family, but that's what living in the Three Mile House for five years had done to me."

"Why then," I asked, "did you ever move from the Three Mile House?"

A long silence followed. Then Doug and Bev very slowly, almost painfully, told their reasons for leaving the place they so obviously had come to love. Bev went first.

"One night, Doug and I went to the movies over in St. Louis and Lynn, with some of the restaurant staff, stayed home. Right away, I started feeling fidgety and anxious during the movie, and couldn't keep my mind on it. All I could think about was Lynn. The more I thought about her, the more I knew something was wrong. I just kept wishing the movie was over. Finally, I told Doug I had to call home.

"Lynn was so relieved I called. She told us that as soon as we left, the spirits had started acting up, but not like anything she'd ever before heard. They began with a banging on the floor that was slow and heavy. Then it got louder and louder until the whole house seemed to be shaking. She was terrified.

"We rushed back home, but the sounds had stopped by the time we arrived. We sent the staff home and later, they each said they felt that a spirit had gone along with them, almost like a protector. That had never happened before. We checked the whole house and everything seemed okay. By that time, we were all exhausted, so we went to bed. But Lynn had a really bad and restless sleep. She woke up with a start when she heard an unfamiliar, deep voice calling her name.

"Outside her second story window she saw a grotesque, oddly shaped green face with piercing red eyes that glowed, dimmed, and glowed again. It was staring directly at her, calling, 'Lynn, come here.' She was terrified, and ran out of her room screaming hysterically. She burst into our bedroom backwards, screaming for help, and threw herself across the room onto our bed. We could hardly calm her down. She was screaming and screaming; it was terrible. She scared the hell out of us. It was the first time anything really bad had ever happened to us in the Three Mile House. For the first time ever, we thought about getting out of there.

"The next morning, Lynn drew a picture of the demon she had seen at the window. We showed it to a professor of parapsychology at Washington University in St. Louis, who said they all look like that. They're green with red, glowing eyes and an odd-shaped head. He didn't call it an evil spirit. He said that it had been conjured up by people who were practicing Satanism in the area, and then didn't know how to get rid of it. Then the demon searches around wherever there's been psychic activity in the area. But there were enough good spirits in the house to keep this one out. That's why it was outside the window. The only way it could have entered the house was if Lynn had let it in. But she didn't succumb when it was calling. The banging in the house earlier had been the good spirits warning us that there was something evil trying to get in.

Bev and Doug Elliot. *"We had really come to love the Three Mile House and the spirits who lived there with us."*

"The professor told us not to leave Lynn alone for two weeks—and we didn't. Lynn never left the house, and we never left her side during that time. After two weeks, everything seemed to calm down, but we never felt completely the same in the house again.

"After the experience with the evil spirit," Bev said, "problems at the restaurant began to multiply. Despite a reputation for fine food, the Three Mile House's country location hurt business when the energy crisis caused the price of gasoline to rise. Illinois' first coal had actually been mined on the property, over a hundred years before, because the house was so large and difficult to heat. Now, with heating bills mounting, the cost of operating the restaurant continued to increase monthly."

Doug told what happened next. "Jim White of KMOX Radio asked us if he could broadcast his annual 'Halloween Spooktacular' live from the restaurant. We agreed, as long as there were no Ouija boards or séances used that might conjure up evil or bad spirits. But one of the guests either forgot the ban or ignored it, because a Ouija board was used, and the result was chaos.

"A loud scream frightened the restaurant customers as the cooks ran from the kitchen, terrified at the sight of a green-faced, red-eyed creature that suddenly appeared in their midst. At the Three Mile House, psychics began to work frantically to drive out the evil spirt.

"After it was eventually expelled and order was restored, we knew something had to be done. We loved the house and the restaurant, we enjoyed the business and the staff—and we even cared about the spirits that we now sincerely believed shared our home. But the rising costs, the exhausting work schedule, and the scary uncertainty of when and where the evil spirit would next appear made us wonder if it was all worth it. We still believed it was, but we knew that it was getting harder, not easier, all the time." Bev told the next part of the story. "As time passed, something else caused us trouble. We had a bar in the basement of the restaurant, and one night Doug felt that he was being taken over by a spirit. He began to speak in an Irish brogue, did an Irish jig, drank a quart of Jack Daniels, and even gave people four rounds of drinks on the house—all very uncharacteristic of him. Someone sent for me, but Doug just told me that, if he wasn't appreciated there, he would go elsewhere. He went down the road to a bar where a band was playing rock music, bought everyone drinks, and demanded that they play something Irish. He then did more jigs, and also taught others, although he had never known such dancing in his entire life. After drinking another quart of Jack Daniels, he ended up drunk at home, not remembering a thing. From that night on, he would occasionally, unconsciously slip into a brogue, and would have to forcefully stop 'the Irishman' from trying to get into him again. By then, too many scary things were happening."

She continued, "The tension, pressure, exhaustion and mounting bills took their toll. We finally realized that we had to sell the Three Mile House. Some of our friends said that the spirits had drained all our energy, but we don't believe that. If anything, we couldn't have accomplished all we did if they hadn't helped us. When we finally left the house for the last time, we were heartbroken."

Doug added, "We had really come to love the Three Mile House and the spirits who lived with us there for five years. On the first night in our new home, I couldn't sleep thinking about all the work, experiences and dreams we had invested in that house. I just tossed and turned and couldn't believe it was all over. Then, and this is the God's truth, I heard the familiar, angelic voice of Sarah whisper in my ear, 'Don't worry, Doug, it's going to be all right.' I didn't understand it all—why everything had happened or why we'd lost the Three Mile House. But when I heard that voice, I broke into a big smile. For the first time in weeks, I slept a deep, restful sleep."

In March, 1985, the Three Mile House burned to the ground. The cause of the fire was never determined, but the building was completely destroyed. Several miles away, the Elliots were safe and sound in their new home and, just as Sarah had said, they were "all right."

THE GHOSTS OF
ST. CHARLES COUNTY

The Blacksmith Shop in Augusta.
"This thing in my shop now is friendly."

*D*oes the ghost of Daniel Boone's wife, Rebecca, still haunt a lonely country road near her gravesite in Missouri's St. Charles County? Is the historic Main Street of the city of St. Charles still haunted by the spirit of murdered abolitionist Elijah P. Lovejoy? These two local legends brought me to St. Charles many times to search for someone who'd actually seen Rebecca or Elijah's ghost. I have to admit, though, I never did find anyone who'd ever seen either one of them. Everybody claimed to know somebody who had—they just couldn't give me their names.

It was after another frustrating day of searching for Rebecca and Elijah that I came across Henry. Henry wasn't a ghost. He was the friend of a man I'd met at the St. Charles County Historical Society. At first, all I knew about him was his name and telephone number, plus an inviting statement: "If anybody knows anything about the ghosts of St. Charles, Henry Evans does." He was just the man I was looking for, and I soon made my way to his home in South St. Louis.

It turned out that Henry Evans had retired from the Bayless School District in St. Louis County in 1976. But his birthplace was St. Charles, where his family could trace its history back for many generations. He smiled as he told me that his father used to joke, "Our family was so old it should be condemned." Then, with storytelling skills developed during a teaching career of thirty-nine years, he proceeded to share his personal reminiscences of a St. Charles childhood.

"When I was growing up in St. Charles, there were many stories about ghosts and hauntings, and lots of tales related about the supernatural. We were always interested about such things because, back then, people used to be terribly superstitious. They were especially frightened of omens, such as a hooting owl or a howling dog. The owl was thought to be the night messenger of death and was attracted to a house where death would soon pay a call. If an owl was heard nearby, people would salt a newspaper and burn it in the fireplace. The smoke was supposed to make the owl go away. Howling dogs would scare people, too. We had a neighbor once whose dog howled all night, and the next morning, its owner was killed in a terrible accident in St. Louis.

"My mother especially had a huge store of such stories. She came from a very, very old German family in Harvester, Missouri. Some of the stories she told us as children, she'd originally heard herself as a child. Today, they must be well over a hundred years old.

"One such tale was about a relative in our family who was dating a lady from St. Charles. Courtship was always done on Sunday evenings in those days. Late one Sunday night, he was riding home on his horse and passed the old Friedens Church. It was a bright night—a full moon—and the church looked as lit up as if it was the middle of the day. All of a sudden his horse became spooked and reared up. He was startled to see a strange old lady in a long dress and bonnet. She was picking up sticks by the fence at the church, and putting them in her apron. Slowly, she turned and thrust a withered stick toward his face.

"He became frightened and, without looking back, fled all the way home. When he got there, he woke his parents and told them what he'd seen. After a long pause, his mother said it was a bad omen. His intended was doomed to die. Within a week, his girlfriend suddenly died, even though she'd always been healthy. He never even had a chance to warn her of the omen that foretold her death.

"Mother always swore that story was true. And when I was a child, it seemed like everybody had their stories of omens, hauntings, and ghosts. Our old family home on Boonslick Road supposedly had one such haunting. About forty years ago, at the time of my grandfather's death, a longtime friend came to pay his respects. After viewing the body in the downstairs parlor, he was urged to spend the night. He'd come from a long way off, and it was very late, but he adamantly refused. Finally, he reluctantly gave the reason—as a young man he'd had a terrifying experience in that house.

"He'd stayed overnight there years before, when the previous owners were away. During the middle of the night, he kept waking up and hearing strange sounds in the kitchen. But he knew nobody was there. Finally, the sounds became so persistent that he went downstairs to investigate. When he walked into the kitchen, he was startled to see a little green man dressed in old-fashioned looking clothes and pointed shoes. He was standing by the stove as if he were busily preparing food, but he did stop long enough to cast a long, hard stare at the 'intruder' in 'his' kitchen.

"The young man became so frightened that he ran from the house in terror. He walked around and around the grounds for a long time, trying to calm himself and logically explain what he'd seen. He finally convinced himself that he'd just been dreaming or imagining. But as he approached the house he felt he was being watched, and looked up to see the same green man walking across the roof and glaring down at him. He never spent another night in the house, even though he was later told by the owners that it was just the ghost of the long-dead Dutch cook who still watched over the house where he had once worked.

"My grandmother used to tell us that she saw 'the little green Dutch man' quite a bit, and so did others in the family. And back in St. Charles, some of our neighbors had the same kind of problems. They had lived in what we called the old Ice House. It was a huge old frame home with foot-and-a-half thick walls, built by a brewery to store ice cut from the river during the winter months. Nobody who ever lived there was happy, and they all moved, swearing it was haunted.

"Our best family friends lived there for a while. They were very respected, stable people, but they were deeply disturbed by the house. Allegedly, one of the brewery workers had been murdered in the basement, and later a young lady who played for the St. Louis City Orchestra was killed there by her own father. Our friends used to be troubled by the sound of violin music playing in empty parts of the house, and nobody in the family played the violin!

"The mother also told us of a large, heavy platter they'd received for Christmas. It was so beautiful, she decided to use it as a centerpiece on their table. She put it down there, but when she returned a few moments later, it had been crushed. It was completely flattened out as if it had been pressed to the table by something very heavy, but nothing else had been disturbed or even moved. There hadn't even been the sound of a crash. No one had been near it, and yet it was broken into thousands of pieces.

"And on snowy nights, someone could always be heard stomping the snow off their boots, but there'd be no one there. The mother was a sensible woman, but she used to run over to the neighbor's whenever it snowed, because she would hear the stomping boots again. Finally, their doctor told them to move, because living in the house was injuring their health.

"Probably the most notorious and famous haunted house in St. Charles, though, was the old Poindexter home on Jefferson Street. It was built in 1855 and, to many, its name was a synonym for hauntings. Lots of

Henry Evans. *"...back then, people used to be terribly superstitious."*

ghosts were supposed to be there. One was a former slave girl who'd hung herself upstairs, and another was a navy man, killed in the Civil War, but often sighted in the house after his death. It was vacant most of the time because, although many tried renting it, nobody stayed for long. The noises, especially at night, were unbelievably terrible. Nobody was able to sleep there. My parents tried to buy it once, but there were two bedrooms upstairs the owners refused to show or even unlock. And the feeling inside was so gloomy and depressing that when they stepped outside, they felt refurbished by the sun. They decided right there never to re-enter its oppressive walls. It was finally torn down in 1963 to make way for the St. Charles Post Office."

Not all the ghost stories were bad, however. Mr. Evans fondly remembers, "One of the first folktales I ever heard was old when I was still a boy. It was usually told me by my German Catholic playmates, and was about the spirit of an Indian that dwelt in the woods around St. Charles. His name was Motauk, and he was an Indian guide who came to the aid of lost children. He was a good ghost protector, almost like a guardian angel, who guided many frightened youngsters carefully through the woods to the safety of their waiting homes. For many youngsters, their childhood belief in Motauk was a great comfort and support during long days and nights spent in the woods around St. Charles."

Near Henry Evan's childhood home is Lindenwood College, long rumored to be haunted by its pioneer-founder, Mary Easton Sibley. Mrs. Sibley is conveniently buried on campus, just a few hundred yards from Sibley Hall, which she supposedly haunts. A visit to the attractive campus found many students who seemed to know all about their local ghost. One co-ed, who worked in the library, shared her version of the tale.

"One of the first things I learned about Lindenwood was that Old Sibley Hall was supposed to be haunted. Up until very recently, it was used as a dormitory, and many of its residents claimed to hear loud clattering in vacant rooms, but investigations found no cause for the noise. Occasionally, furniture would be found rearranged and someone would be heard going up and down the unused stairs. Piano music could be heard coming down the empty hall where Mrs. Sibley's original piano was kept, but the most frequent occurrences were that lights would be seen in the upper stories and attics, parts of the building that were never open, and always kept locked."

One of Lindenwood's best known alumna is a school administrator in St. Louis who remembers a Halloween prank there that went wrong. "When we were students, we always heard that Mrs. Sibley returned to visit school every Halloween. Some said she rode across campus on a horse, and others claimed that she rose from her grave at midnight to walk through Sibley Hall. One year, one of the girls decided to dress up like Mrs. Sibley to frighten the other students. She even got one of the janitors to help her. As she made her way through the great hall, where the piano was kept, she suddenly realized that she was not alone. She looked up, and directly in front of her was an old woman walking with a distinctive gait, dressed in light colors, with a white lace ribboned cap, and curls on each side of her head. The figure slowly turned and revealed the face of the long-dead Mrs. Sibley Then she vanished! The poor girl screamed and fainted dead away. To this day, she insists her weak heart was caused by Mrs. Sibley's 'real' ghostly visit, years before, on Halloween night."

Leaving St. Charles and its ghosts, I decided to drive southwest along the Missouri River, and visit the smaller river towns along the way. It was in Augusta (population 308) that I happily investigated a working blacksmith shop.

After I'd left, I realized that I'd enjoyed my stay there so much, I'd forgotten to ask the smithy if he knew of any local ghost stories. When I returned with my question, he just kept pounding a red-hot metal bar with his heavy black hammer. Finally, the powerfully-built man gruffly answered me with a question of his own.

"Why do you want to know?"

I explained to him that I was putting together stories for a book. But he just kept pounding until he asked me if I believed in "such things."

At this point, I couldn't tell if he was going to throw me out by the scruff of my neck for being crazy, or go after me with his hammer for being dangerous. So I decided to take a diplomatic approach and explained that I'd met lots of intelligent and sincere people who honestly seemed to believe that they'd seen, or heard or felt something that could be called a ghost.

Still pounding, he spat out to me, between flashing sparks, that I'd given him a good politician's answer, but that I hadn't answered his question. He demanded to know, again, with what sounded like total contempt, whether I believed in "ghosts." Remembering my own experience as a child, and all the stories that I'd heard since starting the book, nevertheless I was still a bit surprised to hear myself say, "Yes, I think I do believe in ghosts."

With that, he put down his hammer and, with a broad grin, shook my hand and said, "Then I've got a story for you."

He began with a slow, serious tone. "My wife, daughter, and I lived for four years on a farm in the Femme Osage Valley. The house we lived in had been built over an old stone foundation. The area had been named by Daniel Boone, shortly after he'd settled there, when he saw an Indian woman drown in one of its swollen creeks. History was everywhere we looked. Behind us was an old settlement, but all that was left were the foundations laid up there with limestone. A long-abandoned stagecoach trail of some kind was still there, and along the route you could still find some of the split-rail fences made of walnut. The barn and all the outbuildings were made of logs, and the farm itself had been owned by the same family for over a hundred years. Like most pioneer families, they did their own smithing on the property. At least one of them was buried there, because I found the old grave marker in the barn. But I never could find the grave.

"Anyway, I traveled a lot back then 'cause I was still doing a lot of shoeing, and when I returned late one night, my wife said, 'When you' re gone, it sounds just like the anvil's still ringing in the shop.' The shop was not too far from the house. She didn't say anything to anyone else, just me. Later, though, when I was gone again, my mother-in-law was visiting, and she told my wife, 'It sounds like somebody's still working the anvil.' And my daughter added she'd heard the same thing. She'd come home and be doing her chores and think that I was busily working in the shop. But when she'd go out to see me, I wouldn't be there.

"When I'd be home smithing, I'd see something out of the corner of my eye, but when I'd look again, nothing could be seen. Then something would move in the shop or fall on the floor. And I'd say, 'Well, the wind did it.' It was a small shop, and I had things hanging, and they would sound like someone bumped them. But no one was there but me. 'The wind,' I always told myself. 'It's the wind.'

"I had a boy working for me back then, and he began telling me that he was getting scared because he noticed the noises and shadows, too. He said he was afraid something was going to get him in there. But I just joked that it was ghosts, and left it at that. We both laughed. From then on, though, when my hammers weren't where

I left them, or we heard unexplainable noises, or saw shadows darting about, we'd just joke about it. That usually worked. But when the door began to open and close by itself, the boy quit. So I found myself working alone.

"To me, whatever it was, wasn't anything to be afraid of. It's like it had a personality. Sometimes it seemed angry, oftentimes cantankerous, but always friendly. One night something else happened. It seemed like everything was bugging me anyway. There was a lot of noise in the shop, and things were dropping and clanging. I was in a bad mood, 'cause I couldn't figure out how to make something. I stumbled over some rods and yelled angrily, 'Why the hell don't you leave me alone?'

"With that, my grandfather's heavy ox bow fell from the rafters, hit the floor and bounced clear across the room. After the shop grew quiet again, I said, 'That's all right. I'm not mad at you!' And I thought, 'Now I'm actually talking to ghosts. People will really think I'm nuts.' But since I was having problems working anyway, I said, 'If you're really here, why the hell don't you help me?' And it seemed that just then, I got an idea on how to fix the thing properly. Since then, it has helped me figure out just about any smithing problem. Maybe it's a ghost that used to be a blacksmith. Whatever it is, it's not scary.

"But it apparently became very attached to being in the shop, because when I was moving from there to here, it really acted up.

"That day, I was carrying a heavy iron anvil and was in no mood for long, sentimental goodbyes. Steel rods had repeatedly slipped between my legs and tripped me. Hammers and other tools ready to be carried out had been disappearing. And there had been a lot of loud noises and crashes that had no causes I could see.

"Then, as I was finally maneuvering the anvil the last few inches toward the open door of the shop, the nails of the door's hinges snapped and the huge wooden door banged shut in my face. I was so angry at the point, I just shouted, 'If you want to come with us so damn bad, then come along!' That's when it all stopped at the old shop. When we got to Augusta, I knew it must have followed us, because things started happening here too.

"Actually, it kind of helped me get over the thing that happened earlier. When I was younger, I used to have dreams that always came true. And the dreams were so clear and in such detail, that when they started to happen in real life, I used to try to change them. That used to really scare me, 'cause no matter what I said, the people would continue to say the same words I dreamt, whether my words went along with it or not. Sometimes, if I was sitting next to someone in a vehicle on a long trip, I would concentrate and make them say a couple of words that would be completely out of context. They wouldn't make sense, but they would say them anyway. And I knew it wasn't accidental.

"I told my dad about it. He said it was a gift and that I ought to pursue it. I started studying up on clairvoyance and all that sort of thing and tried to develop my mind. The more I practiced, the more I could do. Well, it got to the point that when there wasn't much to do on the weekends, we'd throw horseshoe nails like darts—at a stick on the wall. When someone threw a nail, I was able to either make it stick, or let it fall out.

"While I was manipulating my mind, it seemed just like when you close your eyes, everything is dark, and you go to sleep. Except, in the back of your mind, a little curtain opened. We already had one person in the family who could tell family members where lost articles were, but this was different.

"When I was younger, I dreamt about a place long before I ever knew it existed. Later, I worked there. And

I knew where everything was before anyone showed me, because I remembered my dream. It was a large barn, nearly twenty horses in it, and an apartment at one end where I stayed with another fella. The dream told me what it all looked like. But it didn't warn me about what would happen there.

"Two days before it happened, clouds came up real quick and lightning struck a large tree at the back of the barn. It split the tree to the ground, but it never did rain that day, just had that one shot of lightning. Next day, Charlie and I were sitting and talking. It clouded up again, came over, and struck a tree on the other end of the barn. Same thing—split the ground open and knocked us both off our chairs. It didn't rain that day, either. The following morning started off as usual about five. That evening Charlie was gone for the night, so, after supper, I just lay down to go to sleep early.

"I was asleep, when all of a sudden, I was jolted awake as if somebody had banged a door. Soon as I woke up, I knew something was there—I could feel a presence. So I got up and looked around, but I couldn't find anybody. I went and looked in the other room. And I searched outside. Maybe someone had come in, and I didn't hear them 'till after they left. But no one was outside.

"When I went back, there was heavy breathing inside. I thought someone was playing a joke on me. So I looked all over the place again, but no one was there. Though I couldn't see it, it was like something was looking at me intensely. All I could hear was the breathing, real heavy, deep breathing. At first, I thought the breathing was me 'cause I was so excited. I held my breath, but it wasn't me. I closed my eyes, but I could still feel it. And it wasn't friendly. It was evil.

"I've been shot at in the Army, and had a knife drawn on me, but the terror I knew right then was worse. My skin felt like something was trying to penetrate it, like something was trying to get into me. My flesh was cold, and I felt like my cells were separating, and that something else was seeping in. I tried to get loose, but couldn't. I have never been so terrified of anything in my life. I felt like I was being held there. Until I finally panicked so bad that I jumped backward and ran out.

"I went downtown to the bright lights and just stayed there. It scared me so bad that I tried to block it out of my mind. Never did go back to work there, but a short time later, the place burned to the ground. The barn was totally consumed in about fifteen minutes. The boss almost lost his life trying to save the animals. Don't know what happened, and don't care. I've tried over the years to think back and see if I did all this in my mind. I don't know whether I did or not. All I know, it was a totally different thing from this thing here in Augusta. This thing in my shop now is friendly. It's actually helped me to get over that other thing." He seemed relaxed as he finished up. "It happens here all times of the day, but it especially seems to favor the dead of night, around three a.m. The town is quiet, but the shop seems to come alive. The sounds are not low to the ground like an animal, but are more like someone walking through the shop and bumping into things. Sometimes big, heavy things start swinging, although they're too heavy to be moved by the wind. And other times the noises become so loud that I can be hammering and still hear them. But they don't bother me. I'm just glad they're friendly. Now, when the lady across the street tells me she could swear she still hears my anvil being worked when I'm out of town, I just slowly nod my head and smile."

LINCOLN COUNTY SUPERSTITIONS

An abandoned house in Lincoln County.
"...people believed back then that if a place was haunted and you tore it down, the haunting would follow you."

Ghosts? Voodoo? Healers? Witches? Haunted houses? Lincoln County has them all. At least, that's what some of the local storytellers claim. Folks in that part of Missouri love a good story. But finding somebody to tell one is almost as hard as finding a real ghost. I haunted barber shops, hardware stores, town libraries, newspaper offices and cluttered auto repair shops before I had any luck. It was finally a librarian in Elsberry, Missouri (population 1,272) who gave me the name of a woman, who knew a man, who had a neighbor, who had a cousin, who just might be willing to tell a story or two. After several phone calls, I finally met my first Lincoln County storyteller.

She was an older woman who had grown up on a nearby farm. Most of her adult life, though, she'd spent living on a quiet street at the edge of Elsberry. She, in turn, volunteered the name of Ezra Tillotson, who had traveled all over the country, but now taught school not far from where he'd been born. Ezra suggested an interview with Mattie Rose Wallace, a woman in her seventies who lived on the same land her family had tilled for seven generations. And Mattie Rose Wallace encouraged me to be sure to visit her cousin Moabious Gentry. Their shared forebears had walked up from Kentucky with an oxcart long before Missouri became a state in 1820.

The storytellers were different in age, education and background, but each of them proved to be uniquely Lincoln County. And most, if not all, thoroughly enjoyed sharing the local superstitions they'd known since childhood.

. . . .

"There are witches in the bible, so why can't there be witches in real life?"

That's how my slightly nervous story lady in Elsberry began—defensively. She looked surprisingly glum and uncomfortable, even though she was comfortably surrounded by the familiar knick-knacks and family mementos of her cheerful modern home. With the delicious smell of homemade Sunday supper hanging in the air, she spoke about witches as naturally as if she were speaking about any "peculiar" neighbor.

But before she continued, she quickly laid out ground rules of the visit: "No names, no pictures, and no tape recorders." Then, and only then, did she cautiously hand over three lined sheets of paper on which she'd carefully written, in longhand, three separate stories about witches. She wasn't about to waste her voice or be misquoted. The stories read:

Years ago, there was always storytelling when friends and neighbors gathered, and the conversation often turned to ghosts, witches, and the supernatural. Witches were a special nuisance to folks, because they liked to cast spells and put their spirits into other beings. But local folks learned pretty fast how to deal with such things.

One such time, a man rushed into his neighbors' home as they were having their noon meal and told them they had a sick cow in the pasture—a very sick cow. Now, the farmer knew his cattle were alright. He'd checked them that morning. And, knowing his neighbor was rumored to be a witch, he suspected it was a trick. They hurried out to see about the cow, but the farmer grabbed his axe as he passed the woodpile. The poor cow was laying on the ground, loudly moaning as they approached it. But when the suspected witch saw his neighbor's axe, he screamed, "Stop! Stop!" Then he ran past the farmer, and kicked the cow. As if by magic, the bewitched animal jumped up and was well. With that, the farmer slowly looked at his axe, and then at his neighbor, who got the message. Sure enough, the farmer never had trouble with a "sick cow" again.

Another suspected witch was named "Lane" (not his real name). One time, he was walking through the woods with a neighbor. When they came to a salt lick, they found a deer feeding there. The farmer slowly raised his gun and fired at it. But the deer just continued grazing. He shot a second time, with the same result. The "witch" just laughed at his neighbor's inability to bring the deer down, or even frighten it. But then the farmer said, "I've got a few tricks of my own." With that, he reached into his pocket and pulled out a silver bullet, and prepared to put it into his gun. But "Mr. Lane grabbed his arm and said, "You'd just as soon kill a man, as not." With that, the deer jumped and ran away. And the farmer was never troubled again with any more tricks from his mischievous neighbor.

Some witches, though, were more than mischievous.

They were just plain ornery. But sooner or later, they got what was coming to them. One day, there was a group of neighbors gathered at a local farm. After lunch, the farmer invited them to come out to look at his horses. He had a number of fine animals, of which he was very proud. The men walked to the yard fence, and the farmer whistled for his horses. One came galloping across the pasture, but dropped dead, right in front of them. The second horse did the same thing. So the man said, "I'll fix that." He ran to the doorway, took his gun and loaded it "real special." Then he aimed at the third horse. As it approached, he shot it dead. Just at that moment, the old washer woman on the back porch dropped dead, too. She was a known witch. After that, witches in Lincoln County must have learned their lesson, because they stopped casting the spells and putting their spirits where they didn't belong.

When I was finished reading the stories, the silence was broken by my hostess. "There are a lot more stories about witches around here, but I don't remember them." With that, my visit was over. After quick thanks, and even quicker goodbyes, I soon found myself driving up the river road to Clarksville, Missouri, to meet Ezra Tillotson.

Clarksville was across the county line, but Ezra assured me over the phone that his story was about Lincoln County. It was winter at the time of my visit and the January sky was overcast and threatening as I drove north along Highway 79, known locally as the Great River Road. In Clarksville, I crossed railroad tracks and bumped down a winding, country road of frozen mud toward the river. The only buildings on the bleak winter landscape were a few river houses built high on stilts. Ezra Tillotson lived in the green stilted house, right next to the Mississippi River.

Ezra was a young handsome man, strongly built, and friendly in a shy kind of way. He quickly invited me out of the cold into a large, warm living room with a picture window that offered a spectacular private view of the frozen Mississippi River. Throughout the visit, he proudly pointed out dozens of the bald eagles that winter and fish right outside his door.

Ezra said he'd grown up in Lincoln County. He'd hunted and fished there as a child, sung there in the Methodist choir, and farmed the same land that his father and grandfather had farmed for many years. Then, after crisscrossing the country hitchhiking, and finally graduating from college, he'd returned there to teach at the local school. It was in the quiet, authoritative voice of a teacher that Ezra Tillotson began his story.

"From the time I was eight or nine years old, I was accustomed to opening up a window after ten or ten-thirty at night and dropping out of it to the ground fifteen or

Ezra Tillotson. *"And I can tell you I know what it feels like to have my hair stand up on the back of my neck."*

twenty feet below. Then, I'd run off to the woods to explore an old log cabin that was supposed to be haunted. I was never really afraid of the dark or anything like that, and never did find any ghosts there. But, to a kid, every vacant house is haunted.

"Later, though, when I was thirteen or fourteen years old, I started noticing a tapping on the walls of my room. Now the house I was born in wasn't that old. But when Mom and Dad first moved to the farm, they lived in the original log house built on the property by Rufus Gibson, around 1840. Rufus was a tough survivor of the Slicker Wars, a local vigilante 'police action' in which one of my ancestors was shot to death, and another almost lost his head with a corn knife. When the logs were originally being raised by Rufus, his boys, and a couple of neighbors, a bad storm came up. Everybody went home. But Rufus decided to stay and work alone. While he was doing that, a log rolled down, crushed him, and he was killed on the spot. My folks lived in his old house until it was torn down. The house that I was born in was built on its foundation.

"Anyway, the tapping on the walls was something I could discount in the daytime. But I had a very hard time discounting it at night. I did finally get to the point, though, that I could deal with it and convince myself that these were just the normal creakings of any house. But the sounds became more and more pointed, until one evening when a friend of mine was spending the night. He couldn't get any sleep because of the noises. The sounds ran outside of all four walls, completely around the room, even though it was upstairs. One of the walls was to the hall, another was to the attic. But the last two walls were the outside corners of the house!" One night, when I was just in that zone between being awake and asleep, I thought I heard a squirrel walking around on the roof, but the footsteps got heavier and heavier as they went back and forth. With a start, I came wide awake. I was extremely nervous, but lay there until it finally stopped, and I was able to fall back to sleep. The next day, I went through all the ordeal of the damned—being frightened, and dreading the night. That evening, the same thing happened again. But this time I jumped out of bed, ran downstairs to my parents' room and grabbed my Dad. I shook him awake and yelled that I was going outside. I ran out and looked up to the roof—but there was nothing there.

"I figured my Dad must have thought I was just having a bad dream, 'cause the next day he didn't even mention it." All I had experienced by that time were sounds, peculiar sensations, and cold spots. But there was more to come. A little later, when I was a senior in high school and my best friend was a junior, we had just come back from a salvage excavation of an Indian mound in Southern Lincoln County. We heard the back door open and close, followed by heavy footsteps across the floor. I thought it must be my father coming in, but it wasn't. It was just between seven and eight, summer dusk. It walked across the hardwood floors in the dining room, so none of the steps were muted. Then it walked up the hardwood steps toward my room. I had decided that it wasn't my Dad's tread but, instead, must be a neighbor boy coming over to play a trick on us. So we hid at the top of the landing and jumped out to scare him, just as the footsteps reached the top of the landing. But nobody was there. My friend and I were both really frightened.

"A couple of years later, when I was away at college, I told my girlfriend about what had happened. In fact, I brought her out to the farm for a weekend, and she was kind of nervous about it. At the same time, since it had been years since the events, I felt I could safely say something to my parents about it without them fearing that I was just a naive or nervous child. But after I mentioned it, Mom and Dad exchanged funny looks. Then they said that before the old log house was torn down, and our present house was built on the site, they'd had the same experiences."

Ezra stood up and paced back and forth across the room. "As far as to whether it's Rufus Gibson, I really don't know, although it sure made me nervous. And I can tell you I know what it feels like to have my hair stand up on the back of my neck.

"There are several more stories I could tell you about sightings that other people had, but folks have said they don't want to talk about them. So I figured I'd just tell you about my own experience." Ezra sat down and continued talking. "I suppose a person could hypothesize about it all, but that's exactly what it would be—just a hypothesis."

The rest of the visit with Ezra was relaxed and pleasant as the two of us talked about eagles, people, and the history of Pike and Lincoln Counties. But before I left, our conversation again turned to the supernatural. Ezra agreed to put forth his own theory on ghosts. It seemed a fitting postscript.

"I think hauntings are caused when something awesome happens in a spot and it leaves a mark. It scars the place, so that something can key it to reoccur. It's even more significant when it's an injustice that's occurred to someone who has an exceptionally strong will, 'cause that someone will keep on trying to make a loud noise about it."

As I made my way across hilly country roads to Mattie Rose Wallace's Lincoln County home, I wondered if her stories would support Ezra's thoughts about ghosts.

When I met Mattie Rose Wallace, I couldn't help but think that she looks like everybody's image of a friendly grandmother. In the middle of Lincoln County, surrounded by several barking dogs, two adult sons, several grandchildren, and several more great-grandchildren, Mattie Rose Wallace quietly thrives. Her home is on the same tract of land that's been farmed by her family for generations. And, although its original 640 acres have been whittled down to just 58, she's hopeful that future generations will hold on to it.

Her son introduced her: "She's heard stories of the last hundred years, handed down from the Civil War to today, and," he added, "she remembers every one of 'em too!"

Mattie Rose Wallace smiled. She talks and moves like a woman half her age, and she's plainly proud of it. She's especially quick to attribute her good memory to being a good listener.

"When I was young, we didn't have radios, or televisions, and all those kind of things. So after supper, in the winter time, when men got in from their work, we sat around the older people and listened. We lived with my grandfather and grandmother, and they had lived back through the

Mattie Rose Wallace. *"...back in the earlier settlements, when people used to live further apart, strange things did happen."*

Civil War. My great-grandparents walked up here from Kentucky. They both came from there and, before that, from Virginia. People talked about what happened back in those days. Of course, we, as children, loved to listen. So that's how it came to me to remember, 'cause we didn't have a lot of other things to take up our minds.

"But the other night, a couple of my great-granddaughters came by, and asked me to tell them some of the old ghost stories—the real ones! Well, in a way, some are real ghost stories, but still they're not. They're actual facts, but unaccountable."

With that, Mattie Rose leaned back in an overstuffed armchair and began her storytelling.

"People today are not so subject to ghosts. They just don't believe like they used to, but back in the earlier settlements, before the country got civilized like it is now, and when people used to live further apart, strange things did happen. Haunted houses were quite prevalent in those days as the Terrell family discovered. They moved to Lincoln County from Virginia before the Civil War. They found a fine house for a good price on a hill ridge about a quarter of a mile from here. Shortly after they moved in, the mother was sitting sewing when she looked out the window and saw two women walking to the house. It was customary in those days when new people moved in that neighbors went to see them, so Mrs. Terrell was not surprised at her visitors. She especially noticed that they had on the prettiest sunbonnets, and thought to herself, as they passed the window, that she would get the pattern. But nobody knocked, so she got up, and went to see what happened to them. But they weren't there. She never did see them again, though she continued to live in the county for years, and got to know just about everybody."

"From then on, though, the house seemed haunted, but nobody knew why. Different things were always happening there. One son was pushed out of the hayloft, and ended up with a broken arm. The father was found knocked unconscious on the floor. So many queer things happened that they finally moved away. The old house was left standing, though, because people believed back then that if a place was haunted and you tore it down, the haunting would follow you."

"So they left the house standing. When my great uncle was a young man, he and his friends would always go out there to sneak up on the house, because at night strange lights could always be seen coming from it. But no matter how carefully they'd make their way up to it, by the time they got there, the lights had disappeared. They never could find out what those lights were about.

"Now down the road is the old Alexander house. It's another place that some think haunted. The only thing I ever heard said by the women who lived there for years was that strange things happened there that couldn't be accounted for. The front part of the house had been built onto the original log cabin. In the summer time the whole house was open and used, but in the winter, they had problems with noises in the back room. Back before the Civil War when slaves were still on the place, it was told that one of them who took care of the children became aggravated and drowned an eight-year-old child in the well. A lot of people trace the strange things that have happened to that occurrence. In the winter, I've heard from others, footsteps and other strange noises could be heard from the back room. One family that lived there started locking the door to the back, but in the morning, the lock would be broken, and the door open. They kept getting bigger and bigger chains, but the only one that held was a heavy logging chain. It's vacant now. The last folks that bought it built a new house. But of course, they left the old building standing."

Mattie Rose continued, "Back in the 1880s when horses and carriages were the main transportation, especially if you had to go very far across the hill, my grandpa's oldest brother walked out to New Hope, cutting across the fields 'cause it was shorter that way on foot. As he came back home, he passed the old Pleasant Hill Methodist Church about a quarter mile northeast of Highway JJ, and then came to the old black graveyard. He noticed a man standing in the cemetery, next to a pile of rails. The rails were used to keep the dirt from falling back into a new grave before it could be used. Now Uncle Willie recognized him as Joe Davis, the old man that lived back of my grandfather's place. Well, Joe was quite a fox hunter. So my uncle thought he was standing there listening for hounds, though he himself hadn't heard any running. It was a bright night, and he went over to speak with him. But the man never answered him or anything. He just stood there.

"My uncle said, 'Well, if you don't want to say anything, that's all right.' But he knew him quite well, and was kind of put out. The next morning, he went over to my grandpa's and said, 'You know, I can't understand it. Last night I was coming back from New Hope and old Joe Davis was standing by the black graveyard, and that old sucker never spoke to me at all. And I tried my best to speak to him—asked him what he was doing. Said I couldn't hear no dogs runnin', but I figured that's what he'd been up there for.'

"Grandpa said, 'I don't want to dispute your word, but I just can't believe old Joe was up there last night. He's been awful bad sick of late and…'

"But Uncle Willie insisted, 'Well, I know him just as well as I know you. It was as light as it could be, and he was standing right there by the corner of the fence.'

"'Well,' Grandpa said, 'It's impossible. They buried Joe Davis in that same graveyard two days ago.'

"Uncle Willie drowned the next year in the Cuivre River. But to the day he died, he swore he saw Joe Davis that night in the graveyard."

Mattie Rose told the stories of her youth with the sincerity of a child. But her faith seemed more rooted in her trust of the original storyteller than in her own personal knowledge of actual ghosts and hauntings. When it came to people with "the gift", however, she knew firsthand what she was talking about.

"Some stories that I heard ever since I was a child were about people that had a special healing power. As I got older, I saw quite a few of these people myself. There was a man who lived in the neighborhood, named Wesley Herrell, and he had the ability to heal the sick, especially children, and babies who were dying. He claimed he had the ability because he was the seventh son of a seventh son. He did it with my own boy, Billy Tom Wallace. All he did was went in and rinsed out his mouth real well. Then he took that baby and played with it till its mouth opened. He blowed into it three times, counted to five, and then blowed into it three more times. Then he said, 'It may look for a day or two that it ain't getting better, but it is.' In three days, that baby was completely well."

"Grandma Huckstep was another healer from around here. She lived down in the Chantilly area. You didn't even have to see her. You could just call her up on the phone. A cousin of mine did that and was well the next day.

"Then there was old Mr. Norton. He could stop blood—would help anybody that was hemorrhaging bad or got a severe wound. And to prove it, one time down at the old livery stable, some people didn't believe he had the power, so they got a veterinary down there, and I know it kinda sounds mean, but they cut a blood vein in a horse's neck, and the old man healed it! When he touched it, and told it to stop—it stopped. The veterinary was there just in case they needed him, but they didn't.

"And there were others. Willy Hammond wasn't a healer, but used to levitate things. He really didn't like to—he claimed it gave him headaches and wore him out too much. One time, he stopped in at the general store in Snow Hill— some folks called it Brussells, but it was originally named Snow Hill. Anyway, the store and town are gone now, but back then, there were some folks who wouldn't let up on Willy. So, finally, he made a heavy table levitate off the floor. Everybody saw it. But one big fellow still didn't believe. He jumped on top and just got carried up with it. After that, most folks just left Willy alone. He died back about 1940.

"Now some said they had the power of the Lord, but none of those folks were what you'd call godly people. It seemed to me, though, that anything like that had to be from the Divine Power. Why they had it, I don't know. Can't say they had faith in God, but the healers did have faith in healing."

Mattie Rose shook her head. "You know, I love to talk about the old times. But it's one of those funny things. Progress takes its toll. It's good in ways. And, in a way, it's not. You just don't hear as much about ghosts and hauntings like you used to. And you also don't hear about the healers and the helpers either. And I think that's too bad. They were a nice part of believing in the old ways."

Mattie Rose Wallace's cousin also has quite a reputation as a storyteller. His name is Moabious (pronounced "Maevis") Gentry. And after I'd finished my visit with Mattie Rose, a quick phone call soon had me headed over to his place for more Lincoln County stories.

Moabious is in his late seventies and is still farming the land his family farmed a hundred years before he was born. In many ways, though, he is still a young man. He and his wife work the farm every day, but when I visited them they were also busy getting ready to move into a new home they'd designed that's built into a nearby hillside, is solar heated, and completely modern. I'd no sooner pulled into his driveway than Moabious greeted me with a big grin and a hearty wave to "come on in."

Once inside his cozy country home, we sat around a kitchen table and settled into an evening of storytelling. Moabious' stories tumbled out, one after the other. And, like the man himself, they were warm, witty, and homespun.

"I've heard of ghosts and hauntings and voodoo all my life.

"And I've collected a lot of stories from when I was younger. I never set them down in writing, but I do remember them. And folks claim that the curse of the voodoo was the worst. Now, I've only had one practical experience with it, and that was told me by my great-uncle Brice. He was quite an agnostic when it came to a belief in such things. But one day, he said an old black man by the name of Uncle Dave Ervin came to see him. Uncle Dave told him, 'You got to come down to my cabin. Old Sally Ann has put the hoodoo on my family and two of the girls are bad sick. If you don't come, and break the hoodoo, they're gonna die!' Now, hoodoo was what the black people called voodoo, so Uncle Brice told him, 'Oh, hell—you can do that yourself.' But Dave cried, 'No, I can't. It's got to be done by a white man who's a stranger to the house.'

"So Brice agreed to do it. He went down, and was shown an old limestone rock. It was about three feet long and eighteen inches wide, and was used for a door step. Dave said, 'Brice, you lift that up, and you'll find a crow foot, an owl feather, and a buzzard gizzard.' And, sure enough, he did find those three articles under it. Then he said, 'Now, you take and burn them, or we're all going to die!'

"By now, Dave's wife and boy were sick, too and the two girls were getting sicker by the minute. Uncle Brice said he was going to get Doc Powell, but Dave begged him to please burn those things first. So he took them out, built a fire, and burned them all up. Then he rushed into town on his horse to get the doctor. But when he got back, the two girls were already dead."

"Doc Powell had a heck of a time pulling the other two out of it. He just never could figure out what killed 'em. But Dave was sure he knew. Uncle Brice never was able to explain it to himself.

"But after that, he always claimed he stayed plenty clear of old Sally Ann."

Moabious leaned back in his chair, with a twinkle in his eyes, as if he were waiting for a reaction. But before I could say anything, he started the next story.

"In the late 1800s, spiritualism was quite a thing in this country. And there were two girls right here in New Hope by the name of Singleton that got quite professional in the handling of the Ouija board. You'd ask a question, and the spirit would rap either one or two, for yes and no. My dad knew them to talk with, and he said that it got so bad from working with it, that they couldn't sleep at night for all the rapping on the headboards.

"But not everybody took spiritualism so seriously. I had two great uncles who lived over near New Hope. One night, when they were playing cards with the other young fellows, they all got to talking about spiritualism. My uncle said, 'All that stuff's nothing. I could perform that.' And they all said, 'You ain't no spiritualist.' But he claimed he was. He challenged them all to come over to his house next Saturday night, and he'd prove it to them. So about a dozen agreed to attend his 'séance'.

"Now, one of my uncles set up a bunch of chairs at the table in the kitchen. And the other, who was a fox and coon hunter, had a big old black hound dog that was real trained. He went to work and had this old hound lay down, and chained him under the table. When all

Moabious Gentry. *"I've heard of ghosts and hauntings and voodoo all my life."*

the boys came in, they had an old, dim kerosene lamp a'sitting on the table. They told them all to sit down and place their hands on the table. Then my uncle said, 'Now I work a little bit different than a lot of 'em do. I have to have the room completely dark.' So he blew out the light. Then he said a few magic words, and gave that old hound a swift kick under the table. Well, the dog started clawing on the floor, and that table started going up. Those boys like to have knocked the door off the hinges. They ran out, grabbed their horses, and left running. They couldn't get anybody back to the house for almost a month."

Moabious roared with laughter at the story. Then he folded his hands, scooted up in his chair, and told another.

"I remember hearing when I was a boy a story told me by Mr. Thomas Davis. He was quite a practical joker, as was his friend, a fellow by the name of Dick Verdear. It happened in about 1885. About nine one night, he and Dick were coming home from a meeting up at New Hope, and up comes a terrible storm. They were passing the old Pleasant Hill Church just at the time it hit. So they tied up their horses to a couple of trees and hurried into the church. The lightning was a' flashing terrible, and the wind was blowing. It just rained to beat the band. So Verdear just sat there for a while, but he was one of those guys that always had to be playing pranks. He just couldn't sit still. So he said, 'Well, Tom, I tell you, while the storm and everything is going on, it would be a good time to call the spirits up out of the cemetery.' So he went to work, got up out of the pew, walked to the pulpit, and started going on. 'Spirits, come forth, and come in the door.'

"Just about the time he got it out of his mouth, the door banged open, and there was a woman, dressed in white, wet hair down around her shoulders, and water all running off everywhere.

"Mr. Davis said his heart went clear through his throat. And Dick turned plain white. Dick stepped from the pulpit. The next thing he knew, he was clear across the room, and knocked a window out of the church going through it. Mr. Davis went out fast behind him. They hit those horses and went home just as hard as they could ride.

"For about a week, they swore and declared that they'd actually seen a ghost. But then they found out that a fellow by the name of George Ball, who lived about three-quarters of a mile from the church, had a sister that had peculiar spells. Whenever a storm came up, or anything of the kind, she'd get a spell and go walking in it. That night, she'd gotten out in her nightgown, as far as the church, just about the time old Dick had decided to go through his motions of calling up the spirits. I guess she heard him going on in there, and opened the door to see what it was. So, although she weren't no ghost herself, she almost created two by scaring them to death!"

Moabious really seemed to be enjoying himself. Each story he told reminded him of another. He cleared his throat and kept right on going.

"And speaking about ghosts, there's a place near here in the woods called Gallows Gap. That's what people call it now, but the real name is Calluses Gap. Named for the old leather suspenders folks used to wear. Back in the time of the vigilantes, during the Slicker Wars, when they'd catch a horse thief or whatever, they'd have a trial. The thief would either be whipped or hung. Well, one time, they went to work after they caught one of those guys over in the Gap. He was wearing a pair of leather calluses, and since they didn't have a rope with them, they bent over a small oak tree, and hung him with his own suspenders. That's how it got the name Calluses, or Gallows, Gap.

"Stories started to get going because people were pretty superstitious in those days, and lots of people believed they started seeing his ghost. After a while, most folks avoided that road near the hollow, 'cause of his ghost and other strange events after the hanging.

"Some time later, though, there was a young man by the name of John Palmer. He was going with a girl he later married, who lived on the other side of Gallows Gap. There was also a fellow by the name of Bill Ferry, who lived in the area and liked the same girl. But it seemed that John was having a little bit better luck courting her than Bill.

"John used to walk back right through the Gap to see his girl. He always took his old shepherd dog that went with him everywhere. So Bill, and some of his friends, went to work. They took a fifty pound white flour sack and caught his dog. They put holes in the sack so the dog could breathe and see. Then they tied it over him. When John started home, they waited 'til just about the time he got to the haunted spot. Then they turned the dog loose.

"The other boys waited at the Gap to see the fun. They said that the dog caught John just as he got to the hanging tree. There was a full moon that night, and he looked back and saw that dog coming down the road behind him. They said, 'Boy, if you'd ever see anybody leave the ground, he did. He never did stop all the way home.'"

Moabious led the laughter. But when it had died away, he said, almost wistfully, "People just don't believe in the supernatural like they used to." Then, with a bright twinkle in his eyes, he added, "And it's just too bad, 'cause you could always have a lot of fun with a good ghost story."

Outside, falling snow had started to cover the roads. It was time to be heading home. In the spring, I'd be back to get some pictures, listen to more stories, and visit again with Ezra Tillotson, Mattie Rose Wallace, Moabious Gentry, and the other good people of Lincoln County.

THE PHANTOMS OF PIKE COUNTY

"Home is where the heart is."

Shortly before I visited Pike County, an historian who is also an archeologist told me, "There's a lot of Indian legends up there about the supernatural consequences that occur if their ancient burial grounds are ever disturbed." His statement led me to Clarksville, Missouri, where nearby Indian burial sites are a very popular tourist attraction.

The Sac and Fox Indians, who once lived and died on the land, buried their dead atop towering Lookout Point. The peak, the highest in the Mississippi River Valley, was also the site of an Indian battle fought to protect the sacred resting place from being destroyed by developers. To the Indians, destruction of the burial grounds meant that their ancestors would be doomed to an eternity of ghostly wanderings.

The Indians did lose. Their burial grounds were destroyed. And now I'd come to check out the Indians' prophecies. The Indian spirits, however, proved to be elusive. But, as I discovered, Pike County was the stamping grounds for a couple of other ghosts who turned out to be real homebodies.

Today, Lookout Point is covered with a large observation tower, a children's playground, gift shops, snack bar, and the open graves of its ancient Indian guardians. Behind one of the cash registers I met Pat and Ray Duckworth, who, at the time, managed the recreation spot. They admitted meeting many fine folks during their busy tourist season—but not one of them a ghost. My visit was filled with a lot of good-natured laughing and teasing, but no ghost stories. At least, not until I was leaving. That's when Mrs. Duckworth asked if I'd be interested in hearing about a ghost from nearby Louisiana, Missouri.

Mrs. Duckworth's story began in 1979, shortly after she and Ray bought an historic vacant house on Louisiana's Georgia Avenue, a street which, with its spacious homes, may well be the most beautiful residential area in the Mississippi Valley. It runs perpendicular to the river, and is an architectural treasure chest. The house the Duckworths bought is six short blocks from the river, right next to the Masonic Lodge.

"We opened it up as a gift and craft center. One day, a husband and wife came in to shop and, I couldn't help notice, they both seemed a bit nervous and fidgety. Finally, the woman came over and volunteered that she'd actually been afraid to come into the old house. Her husband then explained that his wife had grown up in it and, together, they told several strange and spooky tales about the house.

"After they left, I thought about the loud and unusual noises I'd heard in the house. I'd never really paid any attention to them. They'd just been kind of a joke to me. But the repeated sound of the front door opening and closing was a puzzlement. It was heavily laced with bells so that, when a customer entered, they were heard all over the house. Yet, sometimes, I'd clearly hear the door open and close, but no bells would ring. And no one would be there.

"Something else confused me. After the craft shop expanded, the front hallway was used to hang silkscreens. But one silkscreen would never stay hung. It read *Home Is Where the Heart Is.* No matter where, or how carefully, it was hung, within a short time it would be found lying on the floor. I just couldn't get it to stay put.

"The only other thing that ever bothered me was a Christmas basket hung on the mantle. One noon, I was alone in the shop, but heard someone in the front room. When I went to investigate, the contents of the basket had been tossed all over the place. Later, someone joked

Pat and Ray Duckworth.
Their haunted house is now a radio station.

that it was probably just a ghost. But for the first time, I thought to myself, 'Maybe it was.'

"Then, after I returned home from a convention in Florida, all the silk screens of 'Home Is Where the Heart Is' were missing. I looked all over until I found them on the unused second floor. That surprised me. The upstairs was always blocked off so no one would go up there. My son John later explained that he'd noticed them missing, too, and found them tossed around in the upstairs hall!

"I tried putting them up again, but they were continually knocked down, further and further away from wherever I had last hung them. One day, I really got tired of picking them up. So I looked upstairs and loudly shouted, 'I own this building now. And when I put something up, I want it to stay. I know you're here. You can stay if you like—but I want my things left where I put them!'

"After that, everything was left alone, until the shop finally closed for good. The next winter, though, when I was going through the house to check on it, I noticed that one of the doors wouldn't shut. So I put my coat and purse down and went into another room to look for a screwdriver.

"BANG! The door that wouldn't close a moment before slammed tightly shut, locking my keys, coat, money and everything in there. No phone was in the house and, if I left the building, I had no way of getting back in. I found a screwdriver and tried repeatedly to get the door open. But it was tightly locked from the inside. No one was around. As I got colder and colder in the unheated building, I got madder and madder. I became so furious, I took my foot, kicked the door, and it loudly banged open.

"That's when I realized that it wasn't a newly installed latch that had locked me out. It was the original cast iron lock, which hadn't worked for years. The shattered pieces were all over the floor. But I could still read an engraved date on one that said 1850, the year the house was built.

The view upriver from Lookout Point at Clarksville.

"Just then, I glimpsed someone watching me from the outside. As I turned to see who it was, I saw her. Staring at me through the window was an old-fashioned looking woman with long curled hair and a laced high collar. The thought flashed in my mind, 'That stinker locked me out. She's had the house to herself, since we closed the shop and now she doesn't want me to return.' With that, she disappeared."

The house was seldom open after that. A 'For Sale' sign sat on the lawn, and the Duckworth's used it only to store craft supplies. But shortly before they sold it to a radio station, Mrs. Duckworth had one more reminder of her ghostly visitor. During a quiet afternoon visit one day, she heard loud rustling noises in a closed stock room. All the supplies in it had already been carefully packed for their move out of the building. She investigated. Everything in the room was where she had left it—except for one silkscreen. Found loose, and far away from where it had been packed, the silkscreen read, *Home Is Where the Heart Is.*

Close to Louisiana, Missouri, along the Great River Road, are some of the most beautiful mansions in the Mississippi Valley. Many of them sit majestically on the hill tops, looking down on the wide river, which brought great fortunes to their builders and owners.

Years before, I'd seen a huge hilltop home that I'd never forgotten. Since I was in the neighborhood, I decided to stop and ask its owners if they'd share its history with me. They were glad to do so, and even surprised me with a story about a ghost that had come with the house. As long as their names, and the identity of the house, weren't used, they didn't mind their story being told.

"Several years ago, we were driving by and saw this house on the hill. Just like you, we were so impressed with its beauty that we drove up the driveway, and knocked on its front door. We hoped that if we really made a fuss over the house, its owners might let us take a peek inside. Well, we knocked and knocked but nobody answered. Then an old beat-up station wagon pulled up the driveway and parked behind our car. A man got out and asked, 'Are you here to buy the house?'

"We were really surprised. We didn't even know the house was for sale. And we definitely didn't plan to move or buy a new house—especially anything this big. But we were so taken with the fact that it was available that we immediately began negotiations. We spent the next two weeks trying to get it. One other couple had also put in a bid, but they seemed to have lost interest in it. Finally, though, they did end up buying it.

"We were crushed, because by that time we'd really fallen in love with the house. We wanted it so much that we actually decided to move to the area in hopes that we'd eventually be able to buy it. So we bought a house down the road and moved in. We even wrote a letter to the new owners. We told them that if they'd ever be interested in selling, to please let us know. It turned out the new owners kept our letter, but not because they had any intention of selling. They just liked our unusual stationery."

"After two years, we received a telephone call from the owners who said they might consider selling the house. We immediately started negotiating again. After long and very involved discussions, we finally got it. As soon as they sold it, though, they changed their minds. They said they didn't know why they'd ever thought about selling. They liked the house and wanted to keep it. But by that time the papers had been signed, and they reluctantly moved out.

"The first time we went through the entire house, we just couldn't believe how beautiful it really was. Twenty-five rooms, and every one special. When we walked upstairs, and down its long, dark central hall, my wife suddenly turned to the realty man and asked, 'Is this house haunted?' Later, she explained she didn't even know why she'd said it. It just came out. He looked at her, and laughingly played it off. 'Well, if you'd like a ghost, I'm sure we could get you one.' It was only later that we realized he'd never really answered her question."

His wife continued their story. "After that moment, I never really felt alone in the house. The first night we spent here, we didn't even have our furniture yet. We pulled mattresses into the big library and built a fire in the fireplace. We didn't know how to turn the heat up—and it was the middle of the winter! Behind the fireplace, on the wall, were carved faces that stared back at us. During that whole night, they looked like they were glaring at us. It was as if they were mocking us. Every time I'd fall asleep, I'd wake up and see those faces staring through the fire and shadows. I began thinking, *maybe buying the house was a mistake.* There was so much work, and so many rooms. And that strange feeling that we weren't really alone wouldn't leave me.

"During the next few days, no matter where I went, I felt there was always something with me. A spirit or presence, seemed to hover nearby. My husband was at work. The kids were at school. And I was in this empty house, alone—except for that presence. I really became uncomfortable. As much as I loved the house, I never left the kitchen during the day. I brought in a rocking chair, and a television set. Then I'd just wait there 'til the family came home.

"During the first two weeks, more things started happening that made it worse. All houses have noises, but this house sounded like it was crying. There was a real sadness about it. We all found it really depressing.

It was like the house itself was moaning and groaning under the weight of some terrible sorrow.

"And my husband started feeling uncomfortable, too, as much as he loved the place. He got to the point that he never walked through the house at night without turning all the lights on in each room. He kept feeling like someone was bumping into him.

"When we moved upstairs, other noises began. At night, after we all went to bed, we'd hear someone walking up the empty stairway. It sounded like a woman wearing a long dress and high heels. We could hear the clicking steps and rustling sound of her long dress swishing along. She would go past each of our doors, and then down the long, dark hallway. That would happen every evening. But we'd all be too afraid to open our doors to see who, or what, it was.

"One night, my husband woke up, and had dreamt there was a large party going on in the house. In the dream, there were hundreds of people downstairs talking and laughing. But he couldn't make out what any of them were saying. Then he realized he could still hear the party going on. And he was wide awake! He refused to investigate, finally convinced himself it was just a dream, and then fell back to sleep. The next morning, though, at breakfast, our son asked, 'Did everybody hear the big party going on downstairs last night?'

"Another night, we were all awakened by the huge crash of breaking glass shattering on the ground floor. We thought one of the chandeliers had fallen from the ceiling, or that one of the full length wall mirrors had worked its way loose. Everyone ran downstairs. We searched the entire house, but nothing was broken or out of place, not even a small drinking glass. To this day, we still don't know what that noise was.

"And other things happened, too. Once, our son came into the ballroom to turn the light on and found a strange lady standing next to the fireplace. She was beautiful, very young and attractive, but wearing an old-fashioned evening gown. It was a long dress with a white ruffle down the middle. Her hair was in a bun, and she was looking at a flower on the floor. He tried to get a better look at her. But before he could refocus his eyes, she just disappeared. And so did the flower!

"Now he was just a teenager at the time, and couldn't describe a dress if you held it out in front of him. Later, though, in the attic, we found a picture of a beautiful young girl that he insisted was the one he had seen in the ballroom.

"About that time, the town newspaper came out to do an article on the new owners of one of the local landmarks. They even took a picture of all of us in front of the house. A few days later, the reporter called back and asked us if our house was haunted. We asked 'Why?' And he said, 'Because somebody else showed up in your picture who wasn't there when we took it.'

"He brought the picture out for us to see. And there was the woman our son had described. She was just standing at the upstairs window, as clear and distinct as if she belonged with the rest of the family. The newspaper didn't run the picture, or the story.

"After the picture, though, our daughter really became frightened. She told us she wouldn't be as scared if she knew, for sure, that the ghost wasn't going to hurt us. If there was only a friendly sign, she'd feel a lot better about living in the house.

"The very next day, we were all in the kitchen talking about what to do. Suddenly, a heavy wooden chair loaded with our daughter's school books began to lift off the ground by itself. The chair raised about two feet, and then, very gently, returned to the floor. That was the last unusual thing that ever happened in the house. And that was several years ago. We haven't had any kind of problem since that chair signaled us that we had nothing to fear."

Before my visit ended, I asked my storytellers if they had a copy of the newspaper's unpublished picture of their lady ghost. And they did. There she was, distinct and clear, in all her party finery, staring down on the family whose beautiful home she shared in Pike County.

HANNIBAL HAUNTINGS

Stonecroft Manor. *"There are just some things you can't explain, but that doesn't mean they didn't happen."*

The Visitors Guide to Hannibal, Missouri, prominently listed "The Haunted House on Hill Street" as directly across the street from Mark Twain's boyhood home. It seemed a natural place to search for ghosts and ghost stories—but it wasn't. It turned out to be a fun house and wax museum. A very good one, too. But not what I was looking for.

Right next door, though, at the Becky Thatcher House and Bookstore, a friendly lady sent me to the public library to search through the old newspapers for a Halloween feature done a few years before on local hauntings. When I finally found the yellowed *Hannibal Courier-Post* headline I knew I had my first solid lead.

It read: "Spinetingling Tales Recount Chilling Encounters with Ghosts." Laurie Vincent was the writer. A quick call to the *Courier-Post* put me in touch with Laurie and, subsequently, two of the sources for her story.

Within a few minutes, I was walking up Broadway to the Marion County Courthouse to meet Judge J.D. Ogle. He's lived in Hannibal since 1959, and, for the past 22 years, he's served on the bench, traveling between the Hannibal and Palmyra courthouses. Judge Ogle proved to be a friendly, articulate gentleman who was also the first person in Hannibal to agree to share a personal ghost story.

Sitting comfortably in his chambers, next to his silent courtroom, Judge Ogle began.

"As a child, one of my earliest recollections was my mother and father telling this story to my brother, sister, and me. They always told it as the truth. Now, I'm not saying that I believe it myself. But I do know that they sincerely believed it to be true, and that they were very honest people.

"Not too many years before my mother's death, I'd asked her to tell me the story again. I hadn't heard it for a number of years and I wanted to remember it just as she'd always told it. So she told it to me again, and I wrote it down right away so I wouldn't forget. And here's my ghost story, just as I'd written it in my journal, eight years ago:"

Before the days of television or even radio, families used to entertain themselves in the evenings, and one of the most popular forms of recreation was storytelling; oftentimes the stories leaned toward the supernatural. Many were told in an attempt to explain unusual phenomena that people had actually experienced, and most stories of the ghost variety were told as the truth. One such story was told to me as a small boy by both my father and mother who personally experienced this happening. I heard them tell this story many times to many people. It was always told seriously, and as the truth. I'll attempt to relate it here, for my children and posterity. Although, I'm sure I can't do the story justice, the way my father and mother did.

My father, W.H. Ogle, and mother, Ola Mooney Ogle, were married in 1919 and first lived above my father's store, which was Ogle's Cash Store in Rockport, Illinois, population about 200. My mother grew up on a farm a few miles from Rockport, and she was one of 10 children. Their ages were spread so that my mother, one of the older children, was a young married lady when her youngest brother, Tommy, was only 4 or 5 years old.

About then, Tommy became very ill with what I believe was pneumonia. Medical care was almost nonexistent in those days and he was treated at home. His illness dragged on and my grandmother was exhausted from the constant care required. My mother and father helped as much as they could, and would hitch up their horse and buggy and drive out to the farm after closing their store to give Grandmother some relief for a few hours in the evenings. On one of these evenings, Tommy was very ill. Mom and Dad were there until well after midnight, trying to help break the fever with cold cloths and fanning Tommy to help him breathe. Finally, Grandma persuaded them that it was late, and they should go home. They had a business to run, and had to have some rest, too. So they hitched their horse and buggy and started the few miles back to Rockport on the narrow, dirt roads of those days. About halfway home, they were startled by sounds behind them which they described as a sudden, rushing of a strong wind, and the clatter of hooves as of a running horse. They turned to see a small, pure white pony at full gallop pulling a small, two-wheeled pony cart which was also stark white, as was all the tack and harness. Seated in the pony cart was a small boy of four or five who was dressed in white clothing. He was whipping the pony repeatedly and urging him on in words that were audible, but not understandable. As the pony cart overtook and passed Dad's buggy on the narrow road, it was so close that they heard and felt the wheels click. The little boy and cart never slowed, but disappeared on down the road in the distance. Mom and Dad drew their buggy to a stop to discuss what they had seen, and to calm their horse, which had been startled and shied by the occurrence. They agreed entirely on what they had seen in every detail, and especially as to the stark whiteness which was almost luminous, almost a glow. Next morning, in the little town of Rockport, where everybody knew each other, Mom and Dad inquired of everyone they saw and talked with, but none knew of any little boys in the area that had a white pony and a white cart. And what would a little boy be doing out racing down the road in a pony

cart in the middle of the night, anyway? They could get
no news from anybody about any such little boy, pony,
or cart in the entire area. The only news about a little
boy they learned the next morning was that little Tommy
had died during the night, shortly after they'd left him.

"That always kind of gets me. As I think back on the story, I remember my mom and dad telling it so seriously and so sincerely to us kids. I still get emotional when I hear it. But the strangest thing of all was that for years they tried to think of a logical explanation for what they saw. And, of course, they just never were able to find one. They always explained that they were startled by it, but not in fear. The suddenness of it, and what they saw, and so forth was sort of shocking, but they were not afraid. But, gosh, it's a phenomenon that they both completely agreed on. You know, people who fabricate stories usually don't get together like that. So I really believe they saw what they said, and you can take it from there."

I thanked the Judge for sharing his story. Before leaving the Marion County Courthouse, one of the ladies in his office stopped me and asked if I was familiar with the ghost story off one of the highways. She told me of a local legend of two lovers buried in separate, nearby cemeteries, who, supposedly, could be seen rendezvousing on a hillside between the two old graveyards. She gave me the name and telephone number of people who'd built their home on the same hilltop. After a phone call of introduction, I was soon on my way there.

Off the highway, and down a gravel road, I found the house. It was a very long, low, beautifully modern ranch house, and I was warmly greeted and invited in by its middle-aged owners. They proudly admitted they'd designed and built the house themselves. They also readily admitted they'd never heard or seen any ghostly lovers

Judge J.D. Ogle. *"I really believe they saw what they said they saw."*

searching for each other in or around their home, but they did point out the two nearby cemeteries that dated from the early 1700s and 1800s.

Sitting in their large, sunny living room, the lady of the house volunteered, 'There have been two strange instances that happened here, but that was at least twenty years ago. Of course, my husband just thinks..."

"That she'd been reading too many mystery stories."

"I'd been reading mystery stories, it's true, but they weren't ghost stories," she continued. "And I had witnesses.

"I was sitting up reading about one or one-thirty in the morning, when I just happened to glance up and saw a flirt of white, coming out of my daughter's room, as though she were coming out in her nightgown. Then I heard steps going down the hall. The bathroom is between the two children's rooms, and the steps went on past it, so I thought, 'Well, she's walking in her sleep.' She was about seventeen or eighteen then, so I got out of bed to see, but she wasn't there. When I went out, she and her boyfriend were in the living room, and they both heard it, too. They thought it must have been my husband, because the steps were so loud on the floor. But then, the steps just stopped.

"Later the same year, I was clear back on the other side of the house, reading in the guest room. My husband and son were on the other side of the house from me, sound asleep, when I clearly heard someone walking down the hall. The steps came across the slate floor and into the dining room. I thought something must be wrong, hearing steps so late at night, so I called out my husband's name a couple of times, but there was no answer. Then the steps started through the kitchen, which had asphalt tile on the floor, and the sound changed when it came to that.

"Well, by that time, there still wasn't any answer and I was getting a little nervous! So I ran out the other hall and crossed through the house to the bedrooms, but everyone was asleep. Then I checked all the windows, and all the doors, and they were all locked tight. There wasn't a soul in the house, or under a bed, or in a closet! I know, 'cause I checked it all. But it never happened again, and those are the only two instances we've had. Of course, on these slate floors, the sounds of footsteps are pretty plain. They don't creak like wooden floors, so you don't mistake it for that. And we didn't have a dog in the house. Anyway, it wasn't the footsteps of a pet, it was something with heavy shoes on. But if it was a ghost, it was friendly.

"The only other instance we've ever had was when my niece slept over. She swears that somebody came into her room and patted her on the cheek, but there wasn't anybody there. But even that seems friendly to me, don't you think?"

I had to admit it did seem friendly, but I didn't have much time to discuss it. One of the town's librarians had suggested a visit to Stonecroft Manor, a Hannibal landmark built in 1872 that was now open to the public. After Stonecroft, there was still one other contact to make from the Laurie Vincent newspaper article, so I was soon on my way.

Stonecroft Manor is a large, impressive stone house found in the countryside south of Business Route 61. It was purchased in 1954 by Clara Matilda and Carolyn Williams, a mother/daughter team who have restored the badly neglected mansion to its present state of landscaped beauty. When I arrived, mother and daughter firmly denied believing in ghosts, but they also seemed very relieved that whatever the source of the "disturbances" had been, they'd stopped. Carolyn Williams did most of the talking.

"The trouble began when we took out the back wall of the old house. It was shortly after that when we started having problems. Momma was hanging a heavy wooden wall clock in the kitchen when the brass pendulum fell off, imbedding itself upright in the floor, just barely missing her foot. A little later, when we were resting, we heard a loud crash in the kitchen. When we came out to find what happened, the pendulum was clear on the other side of the room, but there was no way it could have bounced that far because it was much too heavy.

"Although there were no further problems with the clock, other 'disturbances' quickly followed. We just wouldn't believe it the first time we heard footsteps. We went all through the house, but we couldn't find anything, or anybody causing them. We didn't believe in ghosts—and still don't—but didn't know what else to think. A number of times after that, we'd hear someone walking in our hall. We'd never find anyone or see anything, but that didn't stop the sounds.

"One night, just after we'd gone to bed, we heard another crash. I was just asleep enough to think someone had thrown a brick through the window—that's what it sounded like. When we got up and investigated, we found a book on the side table in the downstairs bedroom had been thrown to the other side of the room. Now books just don't roll or bounce that far. I pushed it off that table dozens of times, and it just didn't go anywhere. Three books had been on the table, and the top one was the only one thrown. It was a book by Billy Graham called *Angels*.

"Another evening, we were just getting ready to retire when we heard a loud crash in the basement. Momma said, 'I know that's those cartons of freezer boxes I just put down there, but there's no way they could have fallen down. Somebody would have had to knock them over!' We were afraid to go down in the basement, so Momma got a hammer and nails, and just nailed the basement door shut. The next morning, she said, 'Well, are you game to go down and see what happened?' When we finally got the door unnailed and went down, the freezer boxes were knocked off their shelves and were all over the room. All the windows and doors were locked from the inside, and there was no way anyone had been down there.

"As time passed, things always seemed to happen in the evenings, like the pacing footsteps and doors opening and closing by themselves. One night, my niece was visiting, and stayed in the north upstairs bedroom. After she lay down, she heard footsteps that entered her room and walked around and around the bed. She was terrified, but was too frightened to call out. She finally fell asleep from exhaustion. When she woke up, everything was quiet. Of course, she wanted to know if we had been in her room, or if we had heard anything. But the answer to both questions was no."

Since the house opened as a museum several years ago, Carolyn Williams says, "The problem with the supernatural things just stopped." She has no real explanation other than saying: "There's just some things you can't explain—but that doesn't mean they really didn't happen." Of course, she didn't get an argument from me!

A five-minute drive from Stonecroft Manor put me back into the heart of one of Hannibal's oldest residential neighborhoods. I was soon sitting in the large, two-story frame home of Mrs. Mary Wamsley. She didn't waste time telling her story.

"Now what I'm going to tell you is the honest-to-God truth. I'm not making any of this up. This house is haunted. It's over a hundred years old, but we're only the third family to ever have lived in it. And, you know, if I was just imagining these stories myself, it would be different. But everybody around here—neighbors and relatives—know it's true. They've all got stories themselves about what's happened here.

"It all started right after we moved in. My husband and I were working nights, and we'd go to work about midnight. Our bedrooms were upstairs, and we'd take naps before we went to work. My husband, Lee, would notice that somebody was walking up our steps to our bedroom. When he'd go out to find out who it was, there wouldn't be anybody there. This went on for a month, two months, maybe. But my husband refused to believe what he heard. He told me, 'I don't know what it is, but it's not what you're thinking.'

"Then one night, about nine o'clock, I heard a woman scream so loud, it woke me from my sleep. At the foot of my bed there stood a short, heavyset woman and a tall, thin man. Then they just disappeared. She did and he did. Both of them. The next morning, I called the neighbor who used to live next door, and asked her to tell me what the people looked like that used to live here years ago. She said, 'Well, she was short and kind of heavy and he was tall and skinny.'

"After that, things got worse. One Sunday afternoon my husband and I were sitting in the living room and he told me to get the kids out of upstairs. I told him the children were all over at the playground. And he said, 'Mary, I can hear them jumping around on the floor and from bed to bed upstairs.' So I said, 'Why don't you go upstairs and get them down?' But when he went upstairs, there was nobody there, and he asked me, 'What in the world is going on?' I told him 'I don't know but I hear it every day.'

"When my son was about twenty years old, he slept in one of the front upstairs bedrooms. And he kept telling me, 'I don't know what it is about that bedroom, but somebody keeps coming in there at night. They're all dressed in white. I don't know what it is Mom. I scream for you, but you don't answer, 'cause you can't hear me.'

"I thought he was just dreaming, but I have a stepson that sleeps in that same bedroom now. He said that the door between the two bedrooms would open by itself. He'd just say, 'Come on in, you were here before I was.' It kept going like that. He kept saying it, every time it opened. Until one night, about two in the morning, the door came off its hinges and loudly crashed to the floor. He quit saying anything after that.

"Most of the strange things happen upstairs, but it happens in other parts of the house, too. About two or three years after we first bought the house, I thought I heard music coming from somewhere. It sounded like an organ playing inside the house. I got scared. My dad lived right around the corner, so I went and got him. He came over and by then it sounded like the wind was blowing really hard in the basement, but nowhere else. It wasn't windy outside at all. My dad was a brave old codger anyway, and he went downstairs in the basement to see what caused

Mary Wamsley, right, and her youngest daughter, Tylina.
"...sometimes I'm really scared of it and other times I'm not."

it. He said it sounded like somebody was dragging and rattling something—but he couldn't find any cause for it.

"Another time, my sister and one of our girlfriends were in the living room and I was cooking beans on the kitchen stove. When I went to check the beans, footsteps started following me. They walked right behind me, every step of the way, but nobody was there! My sister and friend both heard it. Everywhere I moved in the kitchen, it just followed me. And when I came back to the living room, the steps just stopped."

Mrs. Wamsley's daughter, Virginia, added a story of her own. "One day, we were just acting silly. We were all sitting on the floor in the living room, telling stories, when we started talking about the ghosts and other stuff about the house. Somebody hollered real loud, and everybody jumped up and ran outside. But one of the boys, who was about fourteen or fifteen, was laying on his stomach and didn't move. We were all out on the front porch hollering for him to come on out. But he said, 'I can't. I can't get up.' My older brother, Kenny, said, 'You're crazy. Come on, get up!' and went in to get him. He grabbed his arms and started pulling, but he couldn't budge him. Now that boy was skinny, real skinny, and any of us could have lifted him up—especially Kenny. But Kenny couldn't get him off the floor. Everybody started pulling on him, and finally we pulled so hard, we fell backwards. Then something, whatever it was, released him. He said something was standing on his pants leg, and he couldn't move. And he didn't budge! We'd all tried to pull him up, and none of us could move him an inch."

It was Mrs. Wamsley's turn to add another story.

"One night my husband had a friend over, and I went ahead to bed. But after I was asleep, it sounded like somebody had taken my refrigerator to the bedroom and dropped it right next to me. The men jumped up and yelled, 'What was that?' My husband said, 'Did you break the bed?' But I said, 'No.' I didn't know what it was. And they started looking around the house. I said, 'Wait for me.' But when I tried to get up, I just felt a hand or something holding my shoulder down. And I couldn't move. I screamed for my husband. And when he came in, I was finally able to get up.

"Sometimes I'm really scared of it, and other times I'm not. My sister came down here one day and we were cleaning house. We started upstairs, when she said, 'Let's get a soda to cool off.' It was summertime, and after we got a drink, the racket upstairs really started. You wouldn't believe it. It sounded like somebody was moving the furniture—the beds and everything. So she says, 'Hey, listen, somebody's doing our housework for us!' We both laughed about it. But when we went upstairs, I can guarantee you, it was just like nobody had been there. Nothing had been moved or touched.

"Sometimes, though, it gets so bad that my little girl and I leave to stay with my son until things settle down. In fact,

Saturday night, it got pretty wild, and we stayed with him. We thought when we moved the bedrooms downstairs it wouldn't be quite so frightening, but it's just as bad. The doors open and shut, even when they're locked. The toilet flushes by itself and the bathtub water turns itself on and off when nobody's in the bathroom. None of the women in the family will go upstairs by themselves. The upstairs is pretty much off limits now. But that hasn't stopped anything.

"My brother visited us one Sunday afternoon and we were sitting on the sofa in the living room when we heard a loud crash that sounded like my whole china cabinet fell. He said, 'What was that?' All I could tell him was something must have fallen off the table. He went into the dining room and looked all around. Then he just said, 'I'm getting the hell out of here!' He didn't come back for months. And my niece's husband, who's a great big guy, is scared to death of this house. All of us are, really. My husband says he's not, but I know he hears noises, too, like when we'll be sitting in the living room and hear somebody walking down the steps. We both look up, but nobody's there.

"Lee says, 'Let's go buy a house in the country, or let's build us a new house.' But I don't want a new house. I don't want to leave. I want to stay here. We did move out once, but we moved back after a few months. We just can't stay away. I wouldn't want anybody else living here, anyway. I feel like this is where we're supposed to be, in this house. It's never hurt any of us, and I don't think it ever will. We did have a preacher volunteer to come and sprinkle water in the corners, but I don't think it would do any good. Besides, believe it or not, we're really kind of used to it by now."

GROWING UP HAUNTED IN KIRKWOOD

The Sears House.

"...I've never really felt like we're alone here."

When I pulled up to the house, I noticed an older man, cutting his well-trimmed lawn. It was always a little awkward walking up to a stranger, introducing myself and asking him if his house was as haunted as I'd heard. I never knew what kind of reception to expect. This time, in Kirkwood, Missouri, was no exception.

After my brief introduction was met with a loud silence, the gentleman abruptly turned away and walked into the house. But instead of the sound of a slamming door, I heard his voice call out, "You want to talk to my wife. That's her department."

So I followed him in. He promptly sat himself down in an overstuffed chair, read the newspaper, and ignored me throughout the rest of my visit. His wife, on the other hand, greeted me with a friendly offer to find myself a comfortable chair. Once I was seated, she began in quiet earnest.

"So you want to know about our ghost?"

I knew I'd come to the right place.

She began her story with a flat declaration. "My husband still doesn't believe in them, but I do. Shortly after we moved in, the problem began in the north upstairs bedroom. It was our oldest son's room, but not for long. He said there was something in there with him. But he couldn't explain what it was. And he didn't stay to find out. Our daughter was also disturbed by strange noises in her room, but they didn't seem to bother her as much as our son. Then, when I was alone in the house, especially in the basement, I'd hear footsteps upstairs. And when everybody was home, we'd hear locked doors open and close at night in empty parts of the house. We'd yell, 'Who is it?' We'd go and check, but nobody would be there, and all the doors would still be locked.

But the real trouble didn't begin until 1978, when our granddaughter came to live with us. She occupied the north upstairs bedroom. She began hearing and seeing strange things when she was awake, and having nightmares when she was asleep. One night, we heard the most terrible racket, and ran up the stairs as fast as we could. She was tearing the bed to pieces: Her phone had been thrown across the room, her pillows and covers were thrown back, and she swore somebody was trying to kill her. Later, she told us she thought it was a ghost. She just refused to sleep in that room anymore.

"A friend suggested that we get in touch with a group of ghost hunters, and I did. Five came on a Sunday afternoon, and went through the entire house. They claimed they'd discovered a large, unfriendly ghost in the north bedroom, and a small friendly ghost in the downstairs television room. The ghost upstairs was pinpointed to the area directly beneath our granddaughter's bed. They suggested we move the bed, which we did, and they chased the spirit out of the room. She slept downstairs for another week, but finally moved back up and wasn't bothered for two years.

"Then the whole thing started over again, so I contacted the head ghost hunter. After he came out, she started sleeping there again, with no more problems.

"As for the little ghost, they called him Sammy, and said he was about six years old. We actually became rather attached to him. Occasionally, when small things would disappear, our granddaughter would always say that Sammy hid them. A few days later, they would turn up just where they had been seen last. I even felt we could speak with him. Not with words, but with our minds. He used to come into my bedroom and ask, 'Why is she afraid of me?' or 'Why isn't she here?' or 'Doesn't she like me?'

"Once, at Christmastime, our granddaughter had a boyfriend over. He couldn't understand why she was moving her legs from one side of the couch to the other. She tried to explain that Sammy was trying to get by, but he wasn't amused. And then, when the large Christmas tree seemed to shake by itself, it scared him half to death. She told him that Sammy just brushed against it, but her boyfriend didn't hang around much after that.

"We haven't really had any problems recently. Maybe the ghost hunters got rid of them the last time. They told us that nothing had to have actually happened in a house for it to be haunted. Sometimes, they explained, something might have just occurred in an area, long before any houses were built. Anyway, if any troubles do begin again, they've told us just to call them, and they'd be glad to remove any more unwanted ghosts."

When she finished her story, she suggested I visit her neighbors on Altus Place—the Sears family. Without much elaboration, she told me that they had several stories that might interest me. Then her husband got up to show me out. With a solemn smile, he thanked me for my visit, pointed out the Sears home, and quietly closed the door behind me.

I walked up the steep stone stairs to the Sears house, rang the doorbell, and was immediately swept into the midst of a loud and boisterous family reunion. Several generations greeted me. When I explained the purpose of my visit, delighted family members enthusiastically insisted I stay. Just about everyone had a story they wanted to share about their home on Altus Place.

Mrs. John Sears, the mother of the clan, took the lead, and orchestrated the storytelling.

"I'm not really into the supernatural, but all the stories about our experiences in the house are the absolute truth. Right after we moved here in 1961, I started having problems sleeping. Now, I'm not a light sleeper, and so I don't wake up easily. But every morning at four a.m. I'd wake up to the loud sound of an alarm clock that wasn't there. I'd think, 'Who would set an alarm for four in the morning?' Then I'd realize that it wasn't ours. No one had set it. And no one heard it but me. The only thing that I could associate it with was that we had bought the house from a doctor, and perhaps he always had to get up at that time. Why I'd still be hearing his alarm, I never could figure out. But that alarm woke me up every morning for years.

"And ever since we moved in, I've never really felt like we're alone here. I'm still startled at times because I feel as if someone is standing beside or behind me. But when I turn around, nobody is there. It's happened everywhere in the house, but especially in the basement."

"But even when Mom is away from the house, it's as if she never really leaves it," one of the Sears' grown children added. "Once, when we were all kids, Mom had gone shopping at West County Shopping Center. One of the younger girls had gotten her foot mangled in a bike accident. We rushed inside, and were running water over it, when the phone rang. We were too busy to answer it, but when we finally picked it up, Mom was on the other end asking, 'Who's hurt?'"

Mrs. Sears explained: "When I was shopping, I just got the strangest feeling that something was wrong with the children. I knew I had to call home immediately. I'm glad I did too, because we did end up rushing my youngest daughter to the hospital."

Even though it wasn't the same caliber of emergency, a call from the kitchen ended Mrs. Sears' storytelling. One of her daughters jumped in.

"Just about everybody in the family has heard the slow walking of a man with a cane, treading through the empty rooms of the house. But the worst thing for me was when I was little, and alone, and would hear the footsteps begin. I'd run into my parents' room and lie down on their bed. Then I'd hear voices that sounded like they were talking quickly, while at the same time, speaking in slow motion. It was frightening. The voices sounded like low-toned people, speaking a language that I couldn't understand. It was strange because they sounded like the deep sounds of men talking. But I still thought they came from women because the slow-motion made their voices sound lower. It was like they were speaking a far-eastern tongue, and that made me really scared."

Another daughter added, "I'd always hear somebody walking up the back stairs into the empty kitchen. They'd open a drawer, search for something, and then turn around and walk out again, through the locked back door! I distinctly heard it lots of nights, but nobody was ever there."

"What about the people in the closet?" somebody suggested.

By then, family members of all shapes and sizes were asking for their favorite stories. "The people in the closet" seemed like the people's choice, so Tom Sears was summoned by popular demand from another room. The story was obviously his specialty, and he laughingly obliged.

"One night, I was lying down upstairs and noticed that my closet door at the foot of the bed was wide open. Then I saw a shape that looked distinctly female to me, but it wasn't really clear. It was a shadowy, white figure, who didn't seem to have much relationship with the room that I was in. She seemed to be washing dishes in a room of her own. Just about the time I saw her, she seemed to see me. I lay there, staring at her from my bed, and she stared right back at me from her kitchen! We just kept looking at each other without saying a word. Then, she turned and took a couple of steps away where I couldn't see her.

She quickly came right back; this time she had a man and a child with her. It was as if she'd said, 'Wow, look. Here's something really strange.' They stared at me as if they'd come to see this remarkable phenomenon. They stood there for a long time, and then walked back into my closet, where I couldn't see them.

"And I never did see any of them again, even though they'd been right on the other side of my closet door! They'd even stood and looked at me, on my side of the door! They'd walked right through it, but they didn't seem conscious of it. The walls in their own room didn't match up to the dimensions of my room at all. And the door didn't seem to affect them, or my perception of them. They just seemed to be a regular family with a father, mother and little boy, except they were more like white fog than real people. And it only happened that one time, about seven years after we moved here."

One of his sisters added, "After I moved into that room, I always had problems with that same closet door. Whenever it was open, I'd always get frightened and have Mom come in and close it tight. But when I'd roll over to go to sleep, I'd look back and it would be wide open again. That's when I'd run into Mom's room and stay there."

Tom Sears continued his stories.

"After I moved out of that room, I lived in the basement for a while. One of the lights had to be turned off downstairs by being unscrewed. One night I unscrewed it, got into bed, and it came back on. My first thought was that it cooled, expanded and remade the connection. So I went back and unscrewed it until it was barely hanging in the light socket. Then I went back to bed, and it came back on! I checked it again, and it was screwed tight. So I said, 'Okay, fine. You want the light on? I can sleep with the light on.' And that's just what I did.

Jean and John Sears.

"The worst part for me, though, about living in the basement, was that a lot of times it seemed that the house itself was breathing, that it had its own pulse. A very slow, steady pulse. I swear I heard it: a distinct, slow breath, as if the house were alive.

"And once, when I was down there late one night with some friends, carrying on a normal conversation, we suddenly started talking as if we were brothers in the Civil War. The dialogue was completely out of context, but that didn't stop us. We went outside, and talked about one deserting, and the other coming home and finding his brother with his fiancée. We talked of a court-martial and of the deserter being shot in the shoulder and killed. Then we just stopped. Where the conversation came from, we couldn't imagine. But it was really late, so my friends went home. As they were driving down the street, though, right past our house, they were surprised to see someone run out to stop them. They thought it was me. But then they saw the figure level a gun, as if to shoot them. They stepped on the gas as fast as they could. About five a.m., they called to see if I was all right, and, of course, I was. We never did figure out what had really happened that night. And for several years after that, I had a sore spot in my collar bone, where the Civil War deserter had supposedly been shot.

"It was usually fun growing up in this house, but not always so much fun at night!" one of the daughters volunteered. "Just recently, when Mom was away for the weekend, I was staying here by myself with a girlfriend. We were sleeping on the couch in the living room, but my friend was already scared because of all the funny sounds this house makes at night. Just as I turned off the light, I realized that I'd left the front door open. I rolled over to turn the light back on when I heard footsteps in the room. I waited a little while, then got up to close the door. But I heard the footsteps again. This time they were between me and the door! I thought, 'This is ridiculous, I'm just paranoid.' But the entire time I was walking across the room, I could still hear those footsteps. I even got something in my hand, just in case there really was something there.

"When I closed the front door, the footsteps ran out on the front porch and away. I looked out, but couldn't see anybody in any direction. Then I felt silly to let my imagination get the best of me. I was even a little embarrassed, wondering what my friend thought of my stop and start, ten-minute trip to close the front door. I hoped she was asleep, so she wouldn't ask me what I was doing. But when I got back to the couch, she was wide awake and asked, 'Where did those other footsteps come from?' I really couldn't answer her. But at least I knew that it wasn't only our family who heard strange things that go bump in the night at our haunted house on Altus Place."

A "time for dinner" call from the kitchen cut the storytelling short, and sent me on my way to visit Kirkwood's best known storyteller, Cyril Clemens.

Cyril Clemens, like his famous first cousin, Mark Twain, is a remarkable man. The eighty-four-year-old resident of Kirkwood is a writer, lecturer, editor, and author in his own right, who lives the quiet life of a country gentlemen, in the middle of suburban Kirkwood. His home was built in the last century as a hunting lodge, and is still surrounded by the woods that once covered the entire area. Now, well-manicured suburban lawns nudge up to his wooded lot, and his antique-filled home is a living museum from another age. But Mr. Clemens himself is a very modern man who wasted no time in contrasting the supernatural beliefs of yesterday with the contemporary beliefs of today.

Cyril Clemens at home. *"Years ago it was a true American tradition to believe in ghosts."*

*"...her childhood home in Kirkwood was
haunted by her grandmother's spirit."*

"It's too bad that so many people scoff at the idea of there being haunted houses. Years ago, it was a true American tradition to believe in ghosts. Even today in some cities such as Charleston and New Orleans, they have an appreciation and respect for the supernatural. But people here just don't have the same attitude about superstitions as folks do in those towns. And it's a shame, because a lot of the old stories are being lost forever.

"My own family was always a little superstitious. If you look at my Cousin Sam's writings, there is no doubt that at one time he believed in ghosts. And I still have a very charming cousin in Saint Louis who insists, after all these years, that the house she grew up in on West Pine Boulevard was definitely haunted. No sooner did the family move into that home than strange things started happening. And that's when the house was brand new! The servants began complaining that a strange man was also living in the house. They told of him walking through the place in the evening, stopping at any open doorway, and staring in, as if he were looking for someone. At first, nobody took the complaints seriously, until all the servants quit. Then the new domestics made the same complaints!

"Finally, my aunt sat down and asked everyone to describe completely who, or what, they thought they saw. When she heard their detailed description, she became very upset. She sent for the family photo album and showed them a photograph of the person they described. The servants became very excited, and identified the man in the picture as their nightly visitor. The only trouble was, the man in the picture was her brother-in-law—dead for over a decade!

"He was never seen in the house again, but other spirits supposedly took his place. One was Ruth Stewart, a famous aviatrix of the 1930s. She was a close family friend who gave her dog, Wrinkles, to the children, when she no longer had time to care for him. One evening, the youngest daughter in the house woke up and saw Ruth standing by her bedside. She really loved Ruth but, that night, she became frightened. The next morning, she told her mother, 'I saw Ruth last night, and got scared. I didn't want her to know I was afraid, so I just told her I was awfully tired and went back to sleep.' Later that day, they received the word that the aviatrix had been killed the night before in a plane crash in Pennsylvania.

"My dear cousin insists that during all the years she lived in the house on West Pine, it was continually haunted. The cooks used to tell of spirits flying out the open kitchen windows in the summertime. Sooner or later, just about everyone who lived in that house saw a ghost or two there."

Mr. Clemens chuckled as he fumbled with his pipe and added, "Now I never remember meeting a ghost there myself, but I've never scoffed at anyone who did. My dear, late wife, Nan, though, always deeply believed that her childhood home in Kirkwood was haunted by her grandmother's spirit. Her grandmother was Nellie Custis Butler, George Washington's step-granddaughter. From the time Nan could remember, until she moved away as an adult, she always felt that her grandmother's spirit was in their house on Woodlawn.

"Nan believed that her grandmother would often visit her at night. She would wake up, feel her presence, and then see her standing at the foot of the bed. Usually it was when she was having trouble solving a problem. Her grandmother would come to her and intimate what she should do. Nan always insisted that her grandmother's spirit helped her make every important decision in her life—including whether she should marry me! So you see, I'm rather partial to haunted houses," Cyril Clemens chuckled again. "Especially in Kirkwood."

THE FAMILY GHOSTS OF
WEBSTER GROVES

The house on Plant Avenue. "...*people
didn't stay too long in the house after that.*"
(photo courtesy of Cathy Mueller)

The ghosts of Webster Groves, Missouri, are just like their adopted community. They're friendly, active and very family-oriented. Cathy Mueller should know. She's a lifelong Webster resident who was born in one haunted house there, and now lives in another. I met Cathy and the other Webster storytellers through mutual friends. But Cathy was the only storyteller I'd ever heard of whose story began before she was born.

Cathy explained.

"My mother was pregnant with me when my parents and my older sister moved into our house on Plant Ave. The house was one of the older homes in Webster, and sat on about an acre of ground. It was a big, three-story, white frame house, with a picket fence, and an old barn in the back yard. Right after they moved in, though, strange things started happening.

"At first, there were just small things. Heavy brass wall sconces that had been permanently attached to the walls came crashing down in the middle of the night. Then, they were awakened by the sounds of footsteps walking on the empty stairs. They thought it must be my sister. But when they checked, she was sound asleep. And the family dog started standing in the middle of the living room, with raised hair on its back, barking at something no one else could see.

"My father kept saying the house was just settling, but my mother wasn't so sure. She started to be awakened at night by someone pounding on the headboard and shaking her till she woke up. My father tried to explain it all away, but it didn't help much. The pounding and shaking started happening every night at the same exact time—three a.m. My mother began worrying about what it all might mean, and finally decided to talk with the neighbors about it. They told her the previous owner had died in an upstairs bedroom. During his last illness, he used to wake his wife nightly at exactly three o'clock, just as my mother was being awakened, so that his wife could get him his medicine.

"My mother became convinced that the house was haunted. But my father still needed additional convincing. He got it a short time later, when he was awakened just in time to see something go into my sister's bedroom. It was a fleeting white light that almost looked like passing headlights. But there was no traffic on the street. As the white flash went by, he jumped up and followed it into my sister's room. But nothing was there. That was when he finally started believing that something was in the house with us.

"One morning, my four-year-old sister came down to breakfast and said she'd had the worst dream. She said that a man all dressed in black had come into her room and spanked her. But it didn't hurt. Then he uttered five words to her that she didn't understand. My parents thought that was strange, so my mother again went to the neighbors and told them about what had happened. They really paled when she told them the words, because they were part of a Latin prayer that the last owner had repeated over and over and over again as he lay dying.

"All of these things went on for about six months, and then just stopped. Nothing more. We lived there for another six years or so, but nothing else happened. We eventually moved to another Webster Groves house and, after three months, the new owner of our old house called us. She said, 'You're probably going to think I'm crazy, but things have been happening here that we just can't explain. I'm going out of my mind! Please help us. Tell me if this ever happened to you.'

Cathy Mueller, right, with her sister,
who *"...had the worst dream."*

(photo courtesy of Cathy Mueller)

"Then she told my mother strange stories about what was going on in the house. People, she said, walked up and down the empty stairs, and things moved around in the empty attic. At one point, when she was hanging up wet clothes in the basement, they flew out of her hands, up in the air and back into her clothes basket!

"About that time, Hans Holzer somehow heard about the house and wanted to include it in his book on haunted houses in America, and he did.* The house kept changing owners after that, with more and more things happening to each family that lived there. The hauntings just didn't stop. They kept going on and got a little more bizarre with each new family. People didn't stay too long in the house after that. Finally the last owner didn't even try to sell it. He just boarded it up.

"Years later, my mother heard a knock on the door about ten one morning. When she opened it up, it turned out to be a Webster Groves police detective. He said they were investigating the boarded up house on Plant Avenue, and wondered if we might still have a key to it. They'd been receiving nightly reports of somebody being seen in the house. A figure had been sighted standing at the window on the third floor. The police themselves had seen it when they drove by. But my mother didn't have a key after all those years. Before they left, though, she asked them to let her know what they discovered.

"And they did. When they went over to the house, there was no sign of entry anywhere. After getting in, they searched the entire house. But there was nobody there. Later, when they told my mother about their investigation, she showed them the Hans Holzer ghost book. It quickly circulated through the Webster Groves Police Department. Sometime later, we heard that the house was sold to a

---

*GOTHIC GHOSTS by Hans Holder. Bobbs-Merrill, 1970

parapsychologist who still lives there with his family. From what I've heard, they're perfectly happy and content living there. It seems like finally that house has found the perfect owners.

"And, as for us, the house my family and I live in now has its own story. My mother had a peculiar sense of humor when she was alive. She always insisted that when she died, she'd be back to haunt us. The day of her death, when we returned here, the light in the kitchen started to blink. It went off and on. But it only happened when we were talking about my mother. It would definitely blink. Not all the time, but more often than not. We even started calling the light 'Franny', after my mother. It got to be a big game.

"One night, one of my friends who didn't believe us, came over. She looked at the light and said, 'If it's really you, Franny, turn on and blink for me.' The light blinked! My kids would even be in another part of the house, talking about my mother, when all of a sudden, the light would just go nuts. They'd come running out and say, 'Cut it out, Granny!' And it would.

"We had the light checked. We checked the wiring. We changed bulbs. We did everything possible, but nobody could understand why it was doing that. In about a year-and-a-half, on my mother's birthday, the light suddenly burned out. We put a new bulb in, just as we'd done three or four times since her death, but the bulb has never blinked since. Not one time. It started the day she died. And it stopped on her birthday. I think she was having a wonderful time with it. She always kept her word. She said she was going to haunt me, and I honestly believe she did."

On the opposite side of Webster Groves, near Lockwood Boulevard, can be found another of Webster's "family" ghosts. Its big, beautiful, white frame home is quietly tucked into one of the treeshaded, hometown neighborhoods that have made Webster famous. And its owners are in many ways typical residents, too—except for their ghost.

The man of the house is a well-respected science teacher at a local school, and his wife is a successful career woman. Neither is particularly superstitious. And, although they've come to believe their home is haunted, their attitude about it is very positive and upbeat.

"We never believed in any of this until we moved here. If anybody had even hinted of such a thing years ago, we would have probably just laughed. But after what's happened to us, we don't even doubt it any more.

"A lot of people are curious about living in a haunted house. But, to us, this is just our home. We're certainly not afraid of it. And we're not trying to capitalize on it. We just live with it and are curious observers to what goes on. But, most importantly, we're happy here."

Taking turns telling their story, they continued.

"It all started with the chair. We moved to the house six years ago in July. My wife's father had died in May and we had bought the house just two days before his death. We stored his furniture until we brought it here in November. Then, when we'd come home, we'd notice that the chair would be moved. It would be turned facing out toward the window. How it had moved with no one home, we had no idea. Now my father-in-law had been sick for a long time, and instead of being able to go outside and watch the kids play, he would always turn his chair toward the window to watch them. But that was in our other house. He'd never seen this one. Yet, we'd come home any number of times to find different chairs turned looking out the window. We just found ourselves saying, 'Gee, it looks like Grandpa wanted to see what was going on!'

"The second thing was the television set. Our oldest son had his entire room furnished with things from his grandparents' home. He even had his grandfather's television set up there. His grandfather always liked to listen to the noon news. When he was alive, no matter what else he was doing, he would always drop everything to watch the news at noon. During the middle of that winter, our son's television set started turning on every day to the noon news. It always happened at the stroke of twelve. You'd be downstairs, hear a sound, and realize that it was the TV upstairs. It was always turned on to the news channel, too. Never a game show, soap opera, or anything else.

"Later, we had a neighbor watching the house when we were on vacation. He was a doctor, and very level-headed. When we returned, he told us that everything was fine—'Except, by God, I'd come over and the damn television on the third floor would be blaring!' One day he came over during his lunch break to check the house, and the TV flipped on at the stroke of noon! He said he didn't know what was the matter with it. So I just said, 'Jeez, I don't know either!'

"We'd also find that on the bed in that room there'd be a slight depression, as if someone had been lying on it watching TV. There were twin beds in that room, too, but it would always be the bed with the TV set at the end of it. The pillow would be rumpled, and the bed spread would be messed up as if someone had lain on top of it. It wasn't caused by the pets, and none of the family had been up there either.

"We really tried to come up with explanations because we're natural skeptics. But we never could figure it out. It used to happen all the time. Then it stopped for a couple of years, started again for a while, and then stopped again. Last year, right before the boys were getting home for Christmas, it started again. It's usually centered on the third floor where the boys have their rooms. And it's not just the TV. It sounds like dresser drawers are being opened and closed up there. Doors rattle and even slam shut sometimes.

"One day, when I was working around the house, the two third floor bedroom doors slammed shut. BAM! BAM! It sounded just like someone had really slammed the doors in anger. Well, it was February, so the windows weren't open. There was no draft in the house at all. We don't even have forced air heat in the radiators. I thought, 'Well, isn't that cute!' So I went up to the third floor. Sure enough, both doors were closed tight. Now those doors are always kept open. I opened them again and went back downstairs.

"BAM! BAM! I went straight back upstairs, and opened them again. Within a few minutes, I heard the closet doors in those rooms start to loudly rattle. It sounded just like someone was locked inside. I knew that no person could get trapped in there, but I thought maybe the cat had gotten caught. So I went up the steps calling, 'Kitty, Kitty, Kitty,' but Kitty came following right behind me. By the time I saw the cat, the noises on the third floor had gotten even louder. It sounded like the dresser drawers were being banged open and closed, as if someone were searching for something, but when I got upstairs, all activity ceased.

"About that time, I got a call from school that my youngest daughter was sick. I ran over to school, picked her up, got home, and settled her in bed. Then I rushed to drop off some work, and ran straight home again. When I got back to the house, she didn't answer my calls. I found her standing in the doorway of her second floor bedroom. She was absolutely terrified, peeking around the corner and staring all around her. She was so frightened that she forgot she had the flu. I asked her what was the matter and she begged me never to leave her alone in the house again. She said that as soon as I'd left, the boy's bedroom doors started slamming and opening, slamming and opening. Then their closet door started opening and closing and rattling and rattling. Next, their dresser drawers pulled open, banged shut, and pulled open again. She cried that it just about drove her crazy, she was so afraid.

"It was exactly what I'd experienced earlier, but I hadn't shared any of it with her. I sat down with her, right then and there, and explained exactly what had happened to me, so that she'd know she wasn't going crazy. And I was relieved and glad to know that I wasn't going crazy, either.

"When our oldest son went away to school, his first visit home was the Friday before Christmas. That Thursday night, I couldn't get to sleep because I had a very bad cold. As I was lying there in bed, I heard footsteps in his room, directly above ours. It sounded like one, or maybe two, people walking back and forth, like they were really busy up there. Then his bed would sort of move a little, and its springs would squeak. Pretty soon the heavy footsteps would begin again. Well, I'd gotten his room totally cleaned up, and I figured his younger brother must be up there playing around. I thought, 'I'm going to kill him if he messes up that room!' So I went tearing upstairs and found my younger son sound asleep in his own room. Nobody was in the other room. My daughter was asleep downstairs, and the animals were all accounted for, too. But when I lay back down, the sounds continued for the better part of an hour. It was just like somebody was impatiently waiting for him to return.

"Another night, our daughter had a friend spending the night. Her room was right across from ours. The boys were both out for the evening, but had promised they wouldn't be late. At five o'clock in the morning, I woke up with a jolt to the sound of heavy footsteps pounding up the stairs. They sounded just like a truck. When I looked at the clock and realized the time, I was furious they'd stayed out so late. I ran out into the hall and saw our daughter and her friend sitting up in bed. They both asked who'd just come up the stairs. I told them I thought it was the boys and I was going to give them a piece of my mind! But when I got up to the third floor, they were both in their pajamas, sound asleep. It was winter, and their boots and coats had been untouched since they'd taken them off—hours before. So whoever it was who went up there, it wasn't the boys.

"One morning, after everyone was off to school, I'd gone up and down the stairs umpteen times, passing our hall desk. It's a short writing desk, with storage compartments on either side. When I went upstairs to change, everything was in perfect order. But when I came downstairs a few minutes later, both storage compartment doors were hanging wide open, and all the papers were scattered throughout the hallway. It looked like someone had just dealt a giant deck of cards all over the place. They were all over the hallway, and in the living room on one side and the dining room on the other. The floor was just carpeted with them. Now, who could have done that? The drawers were very difficult to get open, and the papers were crammed tightly into each compartment."

Her husband took up the story.

"The apple tree is probably the most unusual story we've had since moving here. The tree is right outside the corner of the house. It's a big tree, about three stories tall, and bears fruit every other year. One year, it gives a good crop of apples, and the next year, nothing. The first year we were in the house there was a big crop. It was all over the ground. So we picked them up at the end of August. Then, the next year, not one. But the following season there was a mass of blossoms. Pretty soon, little apples appeared and it became absolutely loaded. Then I was away for a couple of weeks and my wife watered the tree religiously. Before I left, we'd asked ourselves how we were going to pick all those apples. It was August, and they were really getting big. We figured we'd have more apples than we'd know that to do with. Then, one night, when my wife was putting away the hose, she thought, 'Tomorrow we'd better pick those apples.' In the morning, she looked out, and not a single apple was left on the tree. No apples on the ground. No broken branches, either!

"About a week later, I came home, and we went out to the patio. My wife sat me down, gave me the paper, and asked if I wanted a drink. It was the first time I'd ever been served a drink on that patio in my life! And I thought, 'Jeez, something is the matter.' All of a sudden I looked up and said, 'My God, what happened to the apples?' All she said was, 'I was waiting for you to notice.' But neither of us could explain it. The apples were totally gone. We knew that somebody would have seen or heard something if kids had gotten up in the tree, especially in a neighborhood this quiet. But we just couldn't figure it out.

"The following year was a non-bearing year, but the next one, the tree was loaded again. This time, we really kept an eye on it. We were planning how we were going to pick them all—when the same thing happened again. All of a sudden, they were totally gone. Not one apple on the ground. Not a trace that there'd even been apples on the tree. If kids had taken them, they would have left the bad ones. Or if squirrels or other animals had done it, they would have done it gradually. But it was so strange, because it had been loaded at eight in the evening, and by seven the next morning, they'd all disappeared. We now have a practice of carefully checking it every single day and night that it bears fruit. But it still happens every time.

"The only theory we have is that we always figured we'd pick apples by sending the children up the tree with baskets. Now, we've done some thinking about all of this, especially with all the things that have happened in our house, most of it related to our children. Years ago, my wife's uncle fell from an apple tree and was killed, and maybe 'somebody' doesn't want our children to be hurt picking these apples. Perhaps they know the danger more than we do. Maybe that's why they all disappear before we can pick them.

The apple tree. *"...somebody doesn't want our children hurt."*

"Anyway, the tree still gives us a thrill all summer. We've stopped spraying and have just given up on picking the apples. We've thought about picking early, when they're not quite ready yet. But they still disappear.

"People have said to us, 'Aren't you terrified to live in the house?' But the answer is, 'No.' We love it here. A friend of ours knew a medium who wanted to come over and exorcise the spirits. But we said, 'No.' If it is the children's grandparents, and they're watching their grandchildren grow up, it's okay with us. Whatever it is that we share the house with, they've never caused us any serious problems, and we'd feel very guilty saying we want them out of here. After all, they enjoy seeing these kids grow up as much as we do. And that's fine with us."

MORE ST. LOUIS COUNTY GHOSTS: FLORISSANT, CHESTERFIELD, NORMANDY, RICHMOND HEIGHTS, CLAYTON, AND UNIVERSITY CITY

University City's haunted (?) house in The Hills.

Ghosts seem to like St. Louis County. Visits to local libraries, museums, newspaper offices and historical societies turned up dozens of haunting tales to add to the stories I had already collected in Kirkwood and Webster Groves. Jefferson Barracks Park, near Lemay, has its legendary ghostly Civil War sentry who, tradition says, appears at times of national crisis. Bridgeton's Payne-Gentry House is rumored to provide a home to over twenty ghostly transients. And in the middle of Ferguson's January-Wabash Park once stood an antebellum mansion that was known locally as "the most haunted house in the county." But it was personal experiences with the supernatural that I searched for, and found, throughout St. Louis County.

Old Florissant's historic Archambault House and another of its famous landmarks, the Myer house, are homes of history and—some believe—of history's ghosts. But the owner of a house, only recently built in Chesterfield, also had a story to tell, as did past directors of Clayton's

Bridgeton's Payne-Gentry House is rumored to
provide a home to over twenty ghostly transients.

Science and Natural History Museum and of the University of Missouri—St. Louis' Thomas Jefferson Library. They believe their institutions have provided hospitality to more than just daytime visitors. On the spot where Ladue, Clayton, and Richmond Heights share a common corner, a retired church secretary remembered her own experiences with a local haunting. And in University City's beautiful University Hills, a prominent local doctor and his family reminisced about the persistent ghosts they shared their home with for many years.

FLORISSANT

My search in St. Louis County began with a phone call to Rosemary Davison, president of Historic Florissant, Inc. She, in turn, gave me the telephone number of her friend, Margaret Archambault, whose pioneer family, a century and a half before, had helped settle Florissant. Miss Archambault's grandfather, Auguste, was a guide with John C. Fremont and a friend of Jim Bridger and Kit Carson. He'd been a famous western explorer and adventurer, known in history books as the last of the

Rosemary Davison

mountain men. Miss Archambault continued the family tradition of living a life of great challenges and adventure—for many years she drove a school bus every day for two suburban school districts.

When I explained the reason for my call, Margaret Archambault quickly volunteered her theory on hauntings. "Your physical body dies, but your emotional desires live on. They're the imprints of life's vibrations. Almost like the afterimage caused by a camera's flashcube."

She also told me that nightly footsteps and sounds of locked doors slamming had convinced her that her grandfather's old Florissant home was haunted. Even its former caretaker, now a local police officer, shared her conviction.

And she knew of another haunted house. "Near Normandy is an attractive, white brick, hilltop bungalow that sits near Natural Bridge Boulevard. It was built by a former governor of Missouri for his crippled son, who lived there his entire adult life. I knew the couple that bought it from the son's estate after his death. They liked the house very much, but they never could sleep there. All night they heard someone walking through its empty rooms. Except, it wasn't just normal walking. It was more like a limping. They were also troubled by what sounded like chains being dragged through the rafters. Locked doors kept swinging open, too. They started studying spiritualism to try to understand what was happening, but the sounds just got worse. Finally, in desperation, one night they grabbed what they could carry and ran out.

"Later, the husband returned to try to pack up some of their belongings. But when he was in the basement packing books, the footsteps started again. Then the basement door opened and there was an old man in full color glaring down at him. The new owner just threw up his books and screamed, 'You can have your house. I'm leaving. NOW!' And he did."

After our telephone conversations, Mrs. Davison asked Margaret Archambault and me if we'd like to meet at her home in Old Florissant. I jumped at the chance, especially because the present Davison residence was originally the home of Margaret Archambault's grandfather.

The beautiful, gracious house rests on the corner of Jefferson and Rue St. Denis, directly across the street from the Sacred Heart Catholic Church, just as it has for nearly a century and a half. Once inside, I sat and happily listened as the two longtime friends shared stories about the historic Myers House, and its Archambault connection. Miss Archambault explained:

"Years ago, before Highway 270 and I-170 converged on its hilltop location, I visited the house because I'd heard my grandfather had known the original builders. The vacant house was threatened with demolition at the time, and was terribly run down. Walking around the

Miss Margaret Archambault

The Archambault House. *"...nightly footsteps and sounds of locked doors slamming had convinced her that her grandfather's old Florissant home was haunted."*

lonely grounds, I was startled to hear a woman's voice clearly say, 'It's a miracle that you've saved this house.' No one was anywhere to be found. And the house was yet to be saved! But eventually it was, and became a Florissant landmark open to the public. Later, it was discovered that Mr. Myers had died before the house was ever completed. Only the cellar and timbers had been put in place, and his pregnant wife had had to finish the house herself. It was not an easy task, especially in 1869. Many people felt a woman couldn't do it. But Mrs. Myers did, with the help of a family friend. It turns out my grandfather, Auguste Archambault, posted the original bond to save the house!

"Since it has been open to the public, many of the people who work there have claimed that Mrs. Myers is still inside the house. They claim they've felt a presence there. Usually out of the corner of their eye, they'd catch a glimpse that indicated it was a woman. To them, she seemed friendly, but a few years back, some workers were putting a new heating unit in the house. They became very nervous, and felt it was unfriendly. They became so frightened, in fact, they even refused to return to the house.

"But we don't feel that way. We're used to it. One night, a volunteer was up on a ladder, painting, and heard the locked front door open and close by itself. Then footsteps walked right through the empty hall. It didn't even bother her. She figured Mrs. Myers was checking on her house. And that was fine with her."

Rosemary Davison then shared a story of her own.

"A few days ago, I was talking with a woman who formerly had a shop in the Myers House. She asked me if I remembered her encounter there with the ghost. She said she was at her desk early one day, when she decided to go upstairs to the bathroom. The bathroom was in a portion of the original porch on the second floor. When she tried the door, it was jammed tightly shut. She just couldn't budge it. She went back to work to wait until someone came in who had a little more strength. Still later, when no one else had arrived, she tried a second time to force the door open. But it still wouldn't move, so she went back to work.

"Then she looked up and saw the door open. A tall woman dressed in black came out. When the shopkeeper saw her, she had no feeling of fear at all—just curiosity. She followed the woman into the hall and then watched her disappear. The woman walked into one of the rooms and just vanished—right in front of her!"

The Myers House. *"...footsteps walked right through the empty hall."*

CHESTERFIELD

Old houses aren't the only ones in the area that have their ghost stories. In Chesterfield, one of the fastest growing regions in west St. Louis County, even new houses can have a spirit or two. At least, that's what a young college student had to say. He called when he heard I was collecting stories.

"Our house was just recently built in Chesterfield," he explained. "It's in a cul-de-sac, and all the houses on the street are brand new. Just a few years ago, the land was just farms, cornfields and grass. Right after we moved in though, things started disappearing, or being moved. For instance, my coin collection just vanished from my room. But the door had been locked from the inside! In order to get in or out, someone would have to tear out the window screens. But they weren't touched. The coin collection wasn't worth a lot, but it never did turn up. And the only way anybody would've known where it was hidden was if they'd watched me hide it, from inside the room!

"This kind of little stuff went on for almost two weeks. Then one day, my younger brother, Ricky, and a friend were alone in the house, babysitting. Our four-year-old sister, Erin, was upstairs asleep. Her bedroom was right across the hall from my parents' locked room. Their room was always locked when they weren't home. Now, when Erin falls asleep, nothing wakes her up. She doesn't walk, talk, or even move until the next morning. Never. But my brother and his friend heard somebody walking around upstairs. They became really scared, and went up there with a baseball bat. They found Erin asleep, but in my parents' room. She was still covered with her own sheets. But she'd somehow gone from her bedroom, across a hall, and through a locked door—which was now wide open. And, she was still sound asleep. Except, now, she was in my parents' bed!

"I came home just about that time, and they greeted me at the front door with a poised baseball bat. They told me what had happened, and we looked through the whole house. But there wasn't anybody else there. We did find all the stuffed animals in Erin's room had been rearranged. They'd been moved from her windowsill and were sitting on her bed and everywhere else in her room. But when she'd gone to sleep, they'd all been in their regular spots.

"Then we found the wildest thing. All the balls from the billiards room were gone, and we found them in the bathtub! The water wasn't running or anything, but they'd all been transported to the bathtub. And that was it. Nothing else ever happened. Later, though, we found out that our house was built on the same spot where an old farmhouse had been. I don't know if that had anything to do with it. But after two weeks, it all stopped. The house in Chesterfield never had any more sounds of footsteps, nothing was ever lost or moved again, including my little sister."

NORMANDY

The haunts of Chesterfield and the University of Missouri—St. Louis both occupy grounds where other buildings once stood. The UM—St. Louis campus rests on the site of Normandy's old Bellerive Country Club. The two institutions may share another link—a type of ghostly practical joker that one of the university's professors calls a 'poltergeist'.

The professor is Dr. Dick Miller, a past director of the UMSL Library, who recently retired from the university. He was described by former students in the Education Department as one of the most popular and admired teachers at the university. After meeting him, I could certainly understand their enthusiasm. Dick is bright, likable, and thoroughly charming. Sitting in his modern office at the university, shortly before his retirement, I noticed that his favorite cartoons were accorded the same places of honor on his walls as several prestigious teaching awards. He has a natural orator's voice that boomingly introduced him as a "born skeptic—when it comes to the supernatural." But through a little-boy grin, he also shyly admitted that his supernatural experience in the UMSL Library had "scared the hell out of me."

"I've been at the university for thirteen years," Dr. Miller said, "and I'd heard stories as soon as I arrived on campus about the lower level of the Thomas Jefferson Library being haunted. The library is built on five levels—two of which are underground. Now, some people said strange things went on down there. And a few of the librarians wouldn't even go down to Level One. Or if they did go, they wouldn't go alone.

"After I became Director of the Libraries, the first day on the job, I took a master key and decided to look over the entire place. I started with Level One, planning to work my way up to Level Five. When I got on the elevator, a lady who was working at the library asked me where I was going. I told her, 'I'm going down to Level One.' And she said, 'Watch out for the poltergeist.' Well, I laughed and glanced at her—but she wasn't laughing. She said people really believed there was a poltergeist on Level One and told of strange sounds, moaning voices, rattling noises, and books falling off the shelves by themselves. Then she said the poltergeist, according to local legend, even came out and played on the elevator at night!

"I just smiled, boarded the elevator, and made my way to the basement. When I got there that first time, it was kind of spooky. It's a long cement room with high ceilings

Dick Miller

and book stacks on one side. I was looking for storage space, so I went through a door into a small room with junk stored in it. Then there was another door that opened to a room under the stairs. Nobody had been in there for a long time. It was filled with filing cabinets, so I started going through them. Then I heard the elevator door open, followed by very obvious footsteps. They walked halfway down to where I was, and stopped. I thought it was my administrative assistant coming to see me. So I came out, looked around, but there wasn't a soul there. Then a strange thing happened. About six feet from me, on the level of my head, a voice just as clear as my own said two words. 'Hello, boy.' It sounded just like a wise-guy parrot.

"Every hair on my body, starting on my calves, all the way to the top of my head, stood on end. I stood there for about ten minutes, and that's a long time to stand still. But I was trying to figure out what it might have been. I first thought that someone was hiding someplace down there to scare me. I thought it might be a voice coming down the ventilation system—but there wasn't any ventilation system per se. I thought someone might have placed a tape recorder down there, but nobody knew where, or when, I was going. So that wasn't it, either. There wasn't anybody there, and no real hiding places, either.

"I went back upstairs and told my secretary and assistant what had happened, then asked them if they'd been down there while I was there. But they hadn't. I made them promise not to tell anybody that the new boss was down in the library hearing voices. They promised they wouldn't tell the hundred or so employees, some of whom were already uneasy about Level One. But within fifteen minutes, everybody know the story.

"A lot of people refused to go down there after that, but my secretary, administrative assistant and I went back down. We reconstructed the whole thing, trying to figure out what physical phenomena might have occurred. But we never could figure it out.

"And so, to keep an open mind, and to look at it scientifically, there are three possibilities. It is possible that it was some natural physical noise in the library that sounded like 'Hello, boy'. The second possibility is that it was my imagination—but I don't believe that, because it was so perfectly clear. And, alternatively, number three is that it was a poltergeist—in which I do not believe. But I did hear something, so I gave the poltergeist a name. I called him Jeff, because the name of the building is the Thomas Jefferson Library. And we still talk about Jeff, the poltergeist.

"One of our library employees was down there alone not long after that. She was bending down, checking some books. Behind her, on a tall bookcase, was a set of heavy, leather-bound law books that had been secure there for a long time. One of them, for some reason, suddenly fell off the top shelf and hit the floor loudly, exactly flat in the small space between her and the bookcase. She said she heard what sounded like a pistol shot, and the next thing she remembered, she was on Level Five!

"Some time later, I talked to the campus cops and casually asked them, 'What's this nonsense about the library elevator hoisting up and down in the middle of the night?' They said, 'Oh yeah, it will be three or four o'clock in the morning, and the elevator will be going wild.' Much later, I was driving on West Drive past the library. I stopped where I could look through the windows and see the elevator light, which showed what floor it was on. The light was going crazy. I sat there a good thirty minutes as the empty elevator raced and bounced between floors. The library was relatively dark. There wasn't anybody in there. It was completely locked. And that crazy elevator was going nuts. When we contacted the elevator company, they told us what we had described was impossible!

"Now, several years later, some of my students still ask me about the poltergeist in the library. After class, a while back, a girl and a boy asked me to take them over and show them Level One. While the girl and I were at one end, and the boy was at the other, a light went out directly over his head. A minute later it came back on. When we got back in the car, he laughingly said, 'You guys should have known better than to play a cheap trick on me like turning the lights on and off above my head.' The girl and I hadn't touched the lights. We didn't laugh. We just looked at each other and shrugged our shoulders.

"Even today, some of my students are astounded that I would ever go back down there. But why not? My greatest disappointment is that when I originally heard that voice say, 'Hello, boy,' I didn't answer it. I only wish I had had the presence of mind to, at least, answer back with my own, 'Hello.'"

RICHMOND HEIGHTS

Playing with light switches isn't an activity confined just to "Jeff the Poltergeist." One of my former students introduced me to the retired secretary of her church, who shared a story about the old Second Baptist Church House on Clayton Road. "Strange things were always happening in our old church house. It was especially bad after dark. Lights would suddenly switch on and off, seemingly by themselves. And doors would open and close without being touched. Lots of people witnessed it, but our poor janitor, who lived in the basement, really got the worst of it. He swore there was someone who walked upstairs all night. He could even hear them talking as they made their way through the house. One evening, it was so bad that he rushed upstairs with a gun. He searched every room, but nobody was there.

"Peculiar noises were heard during the day, too, especially near the large downstairs fireplace. It sounded like someone was building a fire in it. But when I'd investigate, no one would be even near it. I thought it was just me, until the janitor bricked the fireplace up. He was bothered by all the strange noises coming from it, too.

"In November, 1979, a psychic came to speak to the Women's Society at church. Her topic was ESP. After the meeting was over, we asked her to visit the church house.

Church House of Second Baptist Church. *"... people get caught after death and need help to get to the other side. They don't realize they've died because they no longer have a sense of the passing of time."*

As soon as she entered the building, she walked over and laid her hand on the bricked up fireplace. A low eerie sound came down the chimney. That's when she told us that someone had died in the house who hadn't left yet. Next she took us all upstairs to one of the attic rooms. When we were there, she told us she felt a terrible pressure in her chest. She also described a bald, short, stout man who died there of a heart attack. She asked us to pray for him and we did. Then she addressed him directly and said, 'You don't need to stay here any longer. Reach for the light and be gone.' Before leaving, she felt the downstairs fireplace and told us he'd left.

"Then, a few days later, one of my neighbors really surprised me. During a visit, she casually mentioned that years before she'd known the man who'd once lived in our old church house. I was really taken aback. In all the years we'd known each other, I'd never known her to have a connection with our church. When I asked her what he looked like, she described him as short, bald and heavyset. Then she added, he'd died of a massive heart attack up there in his room on the third floor. Her description of the man and his death mirrored the words of the psychic!

"Not long after hearing my neighbor's story, I was leaving the church house, when I looked up and saw a light on in the attic. I went back with the janitor to turn it off. It hadn't been on earlier, and the switch was behind the locked door. I kept remembering the psychic saying, 'Reach for the light.' And all I could think was, maybe this was his way of telling us that he'd finally made it to the other side."

CLAYTON

Ghosts along Clayton Road must really be attracted to light fixtures. Down the road from the Second Baptist Church, a resident ghost was often reported playing with the lights at the Science and Natural History Museum in Clayton's Oak Knoll Park. Local television stations had even featured Halloween stories on the strange phenomena, so I decided to check it out myself. The museum's former director explained how some people came to believe the place was haunted.

"Nearly forty years ago, when the two buildings on the grounds were still private residences, a husband shot and killed his wife in a third floor bathroom. After her death, footsteps, crashes, and loud thuds started to be heard on the floor. Lights up there would suddenly turn on and off and a toilet would seem to flush by itself. Pretty soon, that floor was no longer used. In 1959, the houses were turned into the Science and Natural History Museum,* and the grounds were turned into Clayton's Oak Knoll Park. But workers who arrived early in the morning kept noticing a light lit on the top floor. When they approached the allegedly unoccupied building, the light would suddenly flip off. They'd search the entire house, but never found anyone or anything there.

"One of the museum's original volunteers was a retired army colonel, who was also an ardent skeptic of anything having to do with the supernatural. Early one Saturday morning, before anyone else arrived, he was surprised to hear footsteps crossing the unoccupied second floor. He then proceeded to chase them throughout the empty museum. By the time he finally stopped, exhausted by the chase, he'd become a reluctant believer that the place might really be haunted."

Before finishing, the former director of the museum shared one more story. This one was his own. "Some people heard things. Others saw things. I experienced neither. Although I did feel something I'll never forget. One day, when I was standing in the office talking to my secretary, I felt a hand come to rest on my shoulder. Its fingers grasped me, reassuringly, and I turned to see who it was. But there was no one there. The hairs on the back of my neck stood up, and my secretary said my face turned completely white. To this day, I don't know who, or what, it was. But it was there, and it was very, very real."

When I asked what he thought it was, he didn't volunteer an answer. Earlier, though, my storyteller from the Second Baptist Church had proposed her own theory on ghosts.

The museum moved to new quarters in the former St. Louis Planetarium in 1985.

"People get caught after death, and need help to get to the other side. They don't realize that they've died because they no longer have a sense of the passing of time. They are still wrapped up in their own emotions and just do the same thing over and over again."

UNIVERSITY CITY

Dr. Tony Fathman of University City doesn't really have his own theory about ghosts. But he has occasionally spoken to whatever it is he and his family have shared their home with since 1973. Tony is a respected doctor in the St. Louis medical community, and his lovely wife, Melanie, is an equally respected art historian and instructor at St. Louis University. I'd met the Fathmans through their younger daughter who'd been a student of mine in the University City school system. One evening, we got together in their beautiful home, and Tony and Melanie took turns sharing their many encounters with the resident "mischievous poltergeist."

"We bought the house after its original builder and owner had died," Tony said. "But even before we were completely moved in, we heard footsteps pacing back and forth on the second floor. When we investigated, we found they came from a closed room that was so tightly filled with unpacked cartons and boxes· that there was no space for anyone to walk, or even stand! We blamed squirrels or branches for the noises, but as time went on, the footsteps became more recognizable, and more persistent.

"The next thing we noticed was that commonplace household articles kept disappearing. For instance, once a large box of sponges just vanished from the middle of our empty living room. We never did find them, even though the house was still vacant, and tightly locked."

Melanie continued. "Even before the furniture was moved in, Tony's sister and brother-in-law spent a night in the empty house. But they were awakened by the pacing footsteps upstairs. They searched the whole house. Everything was locked tight. No one was found, but the footsteps continued. After a sleepless night, they'd almost convinced themselves that it had just been a bad dream. Then, as morning broke, the footsteps echoed loudly through the house again. Once more they both searched the house from top to bottom, but the footsteps continued. They never again spent another night in the house."

Tony told the next part of their story. "There was really very little to do to prepare the house for our move, since it had been lovingly cared for by its deceased owner. But Melanie did decide to paint an upstairs bedroom. As she was alone, painting, one day, she had the feeling she was being watched. Turning around, she saw a huge black crow sitting on the outside ledge, staring at her. She went up to the window to frighten it away. But it refused to be intimidated, or even to move. It just continued to stare at her. It was Melanie who finally became intimidated and postponed her painting till another day.

"The crow was seen frequently after that, flying outside the house, or staring in the window at the family. On moving day, a strange-looking little girl knocked at the door. In her hands she carried a large dead bird. It was the same big black crow that had been observing us since we bought the house. She thrust the bird at us, then stopped and said, 'Oh, you're not who I thought you'd be.' With that, she turned around and walked down the street. We'd never seen her before, or since. We still don't know who she was.

"Later, every neighbor we'd told about the strange crow described the deceased owner of the house as a tall, angular woman with strong, piercing eyes, who always wore black.

In fact, they referred to her as 'crow-like', and someone who wouldn't hesitate to check in on her beloved house if she had anything to say about it."

"We were confused about the unusual events since we'd bought the house, but certainly weren't convinced the house was haunted," Melanie explained. "But the former housekeeper had her doubts. She told us of a favorite rocking chair that had started rocking by itself immediately after her employer's death.

"We quickly decided not to share any of these stories with our daughters, but shortly after we'd moved in they started to be bothered by the pacing footsteps and creaking floors. Then their room seemed to fill up with a mist that caused the temperature to drop and chill them to the bone. And Molly, the family dog, who slept with the girls, would start growling at nothing we could see. And her hair would stand on end, too. The girls were becoming more and more frightened. Finally, one night was particularly bad and Tony's anger got the best of him. After putting the girls back to sleep he announced, 'Enough is enough. You're frightening the children. Now stop it!' And it did stop—for a while.

"Two years passed before there were any more problems. But on the second anniversary of our move, the unusual occurrences began again. On a warm June evening, our family minister and several neighborhood children were visiting. Tony took the youngsters out to get ice cream, while our minister and I sat on the front steps waiting for their return. Just as they pulled up to the house, all the lights on the bottom floor went out, and all the lights on the top floor flipped on. Tony said, 'Wow, that was neat! How'd you do it?' But we hadn't. No one was in the house. It had never happened before, or since. The house has completely new wiring, and there is no master switch that turns lights on and off simultaneously. Everybody put forth their own theories, but nobody had an answer.

"After the children went to bed, a neighbor suggested that the previous owner wanted to communicate with us. A lengthy discussion followed and our minister, a neighbor, Tony, and I decided to try something we'd never done before. We borrowed a Ouija board. Then we each asked it what was causing the disturbances in the house. But nothing happened—at first."

Tony explained what happened next. "Melanie was one of the most skeptical in the group. But when she took the pointer, it went wild. It told of many strange things that had gone on in the house. It claimed the house had known much happiness, but also sadness, even violence. The Ouija board said that the bedroom where Melanie had first felt the crow staring at her had been the room where a suicide had taken place. It described a foreign exchange student who'd once rented it, and had taken his life there. But the dead student wasn't the source of all the mischief in the house. That was caused by a mystery child of about seven or eight who'd secretly lived and died there. The child was identified as 'X', but no further identification was given. Its spirit was responsible for most, but not all, of the house's unusual phenomena. The board also explained that the spirits there meant no harm to any of the present owners. By that time, it was getting very late, and the signal was getting weaker. But it indicated that in the future, it would like to talk with us again!

"Well, we were really amazed. We've never been superstitious. We've never believed in ghosts. We've never even seen a haunted house, and had never, ever used a Ouija board. But when we investigated, we discovered that much of what the Ouija board claimed was true."

Melanie brought their story to a close. "Two years later, when June came around again, our bedroom lights began to flash on and off—just like lightning. The surprise was, they'd never worked since we'd bought the house! Even after we'd gotten the whole place rewired! Tony had had an exhausting day at the hospital and said out loud to no one in particular, 'We're too tired to talk right now; try us again later.' With that, the lights abruptly stopped blinking. And we weren't bothered again.

"Now, we're waiting for a couple of more years to pass. Come next June, if we're not too tired, maybe we'll finally get around to the talk we've put off for so long!"

ST. LOUIS' HAUNTED—
AND HAUNTING—LEMP FAMILY

The Lemp Mansion Restaurant.
"...one of the most famous haunted houses in America."

Life magazine once described the gloomy old Lemp Mansion overlooking the Mississippi River in St. Louis as one of the most famous haunted houses in America. But unlike the occupants of most haunted houses, the Lemp family was so prominent in its city's history that its home and its tragedies are carefully chronicled in the now yellowing pages of long-past newspapers.

So before I set out to visit the Lemp house, I went to the St. Louis Public Library to find out what I could about the Lemp family. The reference librarian took a long time before finally returning with a dusty folder of crumbling newspaper clippings. The oldest headline, tattered around the edges, was from 1904.

WILLIAM J. LEMP KILLS SELF IN GRIEF SELF-INFLICTED WOUND IN TEMPLE CAUSES DEATH OF MILLIONAIRE BREWERY PRESIDENT AT HIS HOME ON SOUTH THIRTEENTH STREET

The story read, in part, "Increasing depression growing out of the death of a favorite son, Fredrick Lemp, three years ago, and the death of his lifelong friend, Fred Pabst, the Milwaukee brewer ... is believed to have caused his act." At the time of his death, Lemp's brewery was the third largest in the country and he was described as "the wealthiest, most successful beer baron in St. Louis." He left an estate of over six million dollars—and that in the days before income tax! Faded headlines from 1920 told of more family tragedies:

MRS. TOM WRIGHT (ELSA LEMP) ENDS LIFE SHOOTS HERSELF AT HOME, SUICIDE VERDICT AT INQUEST
Her father also killed himself
Heiress to Lemp Estate

"This is the Lemp family for you!" was how her brother, William Lemp, Jr., was bluntly quoted in the paper when he learned of her suicide. Just two weeks before, Elsa had remarried her former husband, and rumors of her murder were hinted at but never proven. Depression and ill health were finally given as the cause of her suicide.

In 1922, the Lemps sold the brewery they had been forced to close in 1919 because of Prohibition. The seven-million-dollar plant was auctioned for $588,500. Elsa's brother, William, was again bitterly quoted. "How would anybody feel to get eight cents on the dollar?" Six months later, to the day, the headlines told of another Lemp suicide:

WILLIAM J. LEMP KILLS HIMSELF IN BREWERY OFFICE SECOND OF LEMP BREWERY PRESIDENTS TO END LIFE BY SHOOTING
Business Worries and Illness Believed
To Have Prompted Act, Shootings
in Same Building, Former Family
Home, In Which Father Killed Self

The article quoted his son as sobbing over the body, "You knew I knew it—I was afraid this was coming." He refused to elaborate.

The last of the newspaper clippings was from 1949 and reported:

CHARLES A. LEMP, EX-BREWER, KILLS SELF AS DID THREE OTHERS IN FAMILY
Employees Find Body of 77-Year-Old Bachelor
Father, Brother, Sister Shot Self In Earlier Years

A note was found in his room, dated the evening before. It read, "In case I am found dead, blame it on no one but me. *Ch. A. Lemp.*" Nervousness and depression were listed as the probable causes of the suicide.

After learning about the Lemps, I could believe they were depressed. I felt depressed too, just reading about them.

The last article had a photo of the Lemp House. Its caption read, "HOME WHERE 3 IN LEMP FAMILY KILLED SELVES." I stared at the picture a long time. Why would any family stay in a house where it'd known such tragedies? The house itself looked grim and gloomy, which was just the way I felt after putting the crumbling articles back into their old folders.

I kept asking more questions. What must the Lemps have been like when they were alive? Why would people who seemed to have everything kill themselves? Were they so miserable in life that their unhappiness still haunts their home years after their deaths? I knew of only one person in St. Louis who might be able to answer at least some of these questions.

Elizabeth Benoist has written several books on local history. And, as a direct descendent of the founding family of St. Louis, she seems to know the history of just about every important person in the city. If anybody would know about the Lemps, Mrs. Benoist would.

A few days later, Mrs. Benoist and I visited over dinner. As usual, she was plainspoken and to the point.

"The Lemps were truly a family with a dark cloud over their heads. They had everything money could buy except happiness. Young Billy Lemp was my first beau, when I was only ten. But, even then, when they were one of the wealthiest families in St. Louis, they were singularly peculiar and unhappy. In many ways, they were just plain crazy.

"When Billy and I were ten or eleven, we were very close. Later, after we had both been off to school, the telephone rang one day and it was Bill inviting me to lunch. But he'd grown up to be just awful. We went out once more, but that was enough! He'd been the only child of his father's first marriage, and he'd been allowed to just run wild. His father and grandfather both killed themselves. Later Billy dropped dead of a heart attack when he was only forty-three.

"I didn't know his father as well as I knew his mother. She was the famous 'Lavender lady', a tiny little blond woman, who wore lavender all the time. She never wore anything but lavender. She had a lavender automobile and a lavender carriage. Everything was lavender. She was right pretty, but crazy as a coot! She really seemed to love Billy's father, though, but he divorced her. The 'Lavender Lady' was pitiful after that. She just dried up and blew away. She still wore lavender, but she never got over the divorce.

"None of Billy's uncles ever married, but his Aunt Elsa did. She was the wealthiest heiress in St. Louis. Elsa was a pretty blond, but was always unhappy and melancholy. Her husband was a stunningly handsome man—handsome, but evil-looking. He reminded me of Mephistopheles. She killed

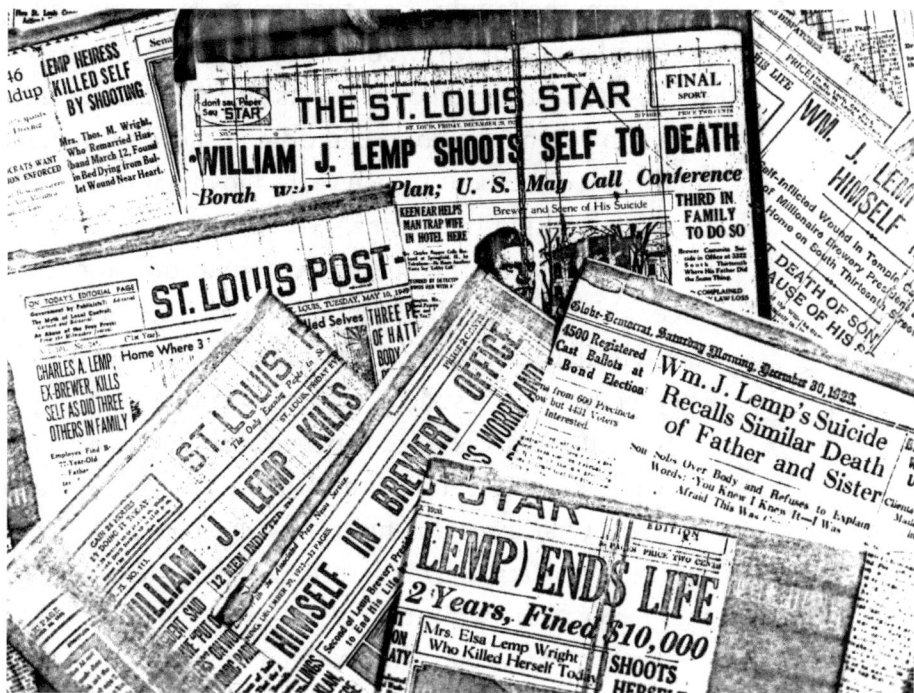

"After learning about the Lemps, I could believe they were depressed. I felt depressed too, just reading about them."

herself in her home on Hortense Place. At the time of her death, there was a grand commotion that her husband had shot her, but nothing came of it.

"Billy's Uncle Charlie lived in the old family home after his father and grandfather had killed themselves there. Now, why would anybody stay in that house? It was because Charlie was nuts! He was nutty as a fruitcake, the craziest of them all. He always wore gloves because he was afraid of all sorts of things. Charlie never took them off. He was very odd and stayed in that old house long after the other suicide. Finally, he killed himself in there, too.

"Eddie Lemp, another of Billy's uncles, didn't stay in the house. He was less crazy than the other ones, but he was odd, too. At least he was smart enough, though, to get away from the family—and that house. He owned a big, beautiful estate in Kirkwood, but he was afraid to be left alone. He always had house guests and kept his servants with him around the clock. Eddie didn't shoot himself. He finally just died about fifteen years ago of natural causes. He was the last of the Lemps.

"The family, like their brewery, is gone now. Somebody once said that if they had kept up and paid attention to it, they'd be like the Busch family today. But they let it slide. They let everything slide. They just didn't care.

"And that house is still down there, supposedly haunted. Well, if it is haunted, then I think it must be the 'Lavender Lady' and Charlie that haunt it. They were both so unhappy, maybe they're still down there, looking for the happiness they never found while they were alive."

Liz Benoist, as usual, hadn't minced words. I felt as if I knew the Lemps a little better. But I still hadn't visited the old Lemp mansion which is now a restaurant. Just about that time though, one of the players on the soccer team I coached, told me his brother, Claude, had helped restore the Lemp house. Claude had never believed in ghosts before, but his experience at the Lemp place had changed his mind. That was all I needed to know. I called him up and we agreed to meet.

Claude Breckwoldt is a young, talented professional painter who emigrated from South Africa when he was just a boy. After graduating from the St. Louis University Art School, he's helped restore old homes in Compton Heights, Portland Place, and other historic St. Louis neighborhoods. Claude told me, "I've worked in many old mansions, all by myself, and late at night. And I've never been frightened, until I worked at the Lemp house."

He explained: "At first, the house seemed pretty friendly. I'd just walk in and paint away. I'd never really heard any of the strange stories about the place. A couple

Claude Breckwoldt.

"...all I could think of was that I had to get out of there."

of times, I even worked late at night, but not too late. When it got dark, I usually quit.

"The one night that really creeped me, though, was a Monday when the new restaurant they'd opened in the basement was closed. The owner said, 'Let's try to finish this all up.' So I figured if I worked a really long night, I could do it. I was up there on my scaffold about nine or ten o'clock just working away, when I got this feeling. It was like you were at a ball game and pinpointed one person in the crowd and just kept staring at him. Before long, he'd turn around and make eye contact with you. It was that kind of sensation, but I was the one being watched! I knew there was nobody else in the house, but I could still feel the staring.

"I kept thinking, 'God, I'm too old for this. This is just crazy!' I was trying to work, and not to think about it. But I couldn't get rid of those feelings. My hairs were almost on end. I live in an old house myself, and never felt anything like that feeling. So that just made it worse. I tried to keep going, but after about ten or fifteen minutes, all I could think of was that I had to get out of there. For the first time in my life, I was scared out of a house.

"I got off the scaffold but, behind every door, I kept expecting to come face to face with whatever was staring at me. I couldn't get over the feeling that someone was watching my every movement. I went down the passageway to the basement which was the way out. Not a single light was on down there, just black, pitch black. When I saw how dark it was, I turned around to get out the locked front door. By that time, all I could think about was, 'Man, let me outta here!' Somehow I got the door open and ran straight across the street to where the owners of the restaurant lived. I told them, that was it for tonight. They'd have to go back and lock the doors themselves."

Claude continued, "I don't really believe too much in ghosts, but there was something there. It was not a being,

The Lavender Lady. *"She was right pretty, but crazy as a coot."*

a ghost maybe, but whatever it was, it was something almost evil. The only other time I felt like that was when I was a little kid at night, and I thought my sweater or something in the room was going to get me. It really gave me the willies. It definitely is a creepy house. I think some houses just have bad vibrations because bad families have lived there, or bad things have happened there. The Lemp mansion is one of those houses."

It was time for me to visit the Lemp house myself. As I drove down Highway 55, I passed the huge Anheuser-Busch Brewery, which was humming with activity. Turning off the next exit, I came face-to-face with the boarded-up and still-vacant Lemp Brewery, empty and silent after 65 years. It was hard to imagine that once the Lemps had dominated the brewing industry, just as the Busch family does today. Sitting in the shadows between the locked Lemp Brewery and its triumphant rival, Anheuser-Busch, is the Lemp Mansion Restaurant. The house looked just as grey and gloomy as it had in the now-faded newspaper picture taken at the time of the last Lemp suicide. To me, it was starkly ugly.

But when Dick Pointer, the current owner, answered the front door, he was all smiles. It was Saturday morning, and the restaurant was closed. So Mr. Pointer was able to spend some time talking about the Lemps, the house and its supposed hauntings. The house is attractively decorated. But even on a bright day, it seemed dark inside. Dick took me into a side dining room. Sitting underneath a portrait of a woman who could only be the famous "Lavender Lady", he told the Lemps' story.

"The Lemps were crazy. Their troubles seemed to begin with the death of a son. That was Fred. He helped to build the brewery, and was a real wizard in regards to marketing and promotion. We found a poster that showed a woman revealing her pointed, high-button shoe. It read,

'Women also drink Lemp Beer.' That was Fredrick Lemp's idea. It caused him to be thrown out of the Leaders Club for introducing ladies and sexism into advertising. Most people didn't like that at the turn of the century, but it sold beer. He was William Lemp's favorite son, and died suddenly when he was only twenty-eight. His father never got over his death and killed himself in this room. William Lemp, Jr. also killed himself here. That's why we call it the 'suicide room'.

"The 'Lavender Lady' was William Lemp, Jr.'s first wife. They had a stormy marriage, and an even stormier divorce. He probably wanted to divorce her because she was as crazy as he was. People called her 'Lavender Lil'. All of her clothes were lavender, and so was her carriage. Her horse even had lavender leather! Every morning she was given a thousand dollar bill, and a promise. If she didn't spend it all, the next day she wouldn't get any!

"During the divorce trial, it came out that William had tried to run over people he didn't like with his horse and carriage. He also used to shoot guns over people's heads, to frighten them. But the 'Lavender Lady' still lost the case. She admitted on the stand that she smoked cigarettes. In those days, that was considered even more scandalous, and public opinion turned against her.

"But Lemp was nuts, too! He kept twelve million in cash in three bank vaults he built at home because he didn't trust public banks. And to avoid contact with people, he walked to work through caves that connected his house with the brewery. The house was built over the largest natural cave formations under any city in America. That's why the German brewers came here in the first place. They put ice in the caves to cool their beer. And Lemp owned the largest, and best, caves underneath St. Louis. He loved it down there, and even built a swimming pool, ball room, and vaudeville stage underground. It's all still there, right under Cherokee Street, but now it's rotted and moldy. They were crazy all right. By our standards, or anybody else's."

As we sat in the "suicide room", I tried to imagine what the caves looked like today, and how they must have looked at one time. Dick Pointer said he had never really explored them because he was still busy trying to restore the house itself. That caused me to ask how he had actually come to own the Lemp House. He explained.

"We came down this way to visit the DeMenil House, and ended up parking in front of an old hitching post shaped like a beer bottle. That seemed strange. Then I realized this must be the Lemp house. I'd seen it written up a few years before in a newspaper article that told all about the family suicides and tragedies. The story was about the rise and fall of the Lemps and how their dynasty and business fortune declined until their old home had actually become a slum rooming house. And in 1975, that's exactly what it was!

"I told my son that this would make a tremendous place for a restaurant. We went in and looked around. All the big rooms had been subdivided and partitioned. The high fresco ceilings were covered with ugly paint. And everywhere we looked, we found darkness and strange people. It was full of all the usual things found in any rundown slum.

"As soon as I walked in, I had a funny sensation, but just figured it was because of the way everything looked. We found an application for a rooming house license on the wall, and copied the name of the owner, and his telephone number. We called him up, made an offer, and that's how we ended up buying the place.

"Once we started moving walls and things to get it all back to its original structure, I noticed strange feelings when I was alone here late at night. One evening in particular, I was painting the bathroom when I felt

Dick Pointer. *"Psychics from as far away as Los Angeles have visited and left convinced this place is haunted."*

someone staring at me. I guess we all have a sixth sense to know when somebody is watching us. I turned to the door, because that's where I felt him. I figured my son was back from his ball game, so I called his name. No answer. I called him again, but the house was filled with silence. I started getting aggravated, because I knew somebody was there, and thought they were trying to play a trick on me. I yelled out, 'Come on. Don't play around. If you're here, help me paint!' Then I looked all through the building, but couldn't find anybody. Every door and window was locked. Nobody was in the house but me. I thought, 'My God, I'm just scaring myself.' So I went back to painting.

"Five minutes later, I was even more scared. I felt a tremendous sensation of somebody watching me again. I put the paint brush down, closed up the paint and was out the back door! Several others experienced the same thing, and one guy even had a stranger experience.

"He was from southern California, and lived in the house while he was painting the front room. Every morning he came downstairs and told us he'd heard horses in the yard during the night. He said the horses came out of the old carriage house, and walked around the cobblestoned courtyard right underneath his window. At the time, he was staying in the 'Lavender Lady's' old bedroom on the second floor. From the window you could clearly see the old carriage house entrance, and the grass side yard. But there was no cobblestone courtyard! This went on for a couple of weeks, with him insisting that he heard the horses every night, right after midnight. It really got to be a sore spot between us. I always tried to explain it away, and he'd just get angrier and angrier. Finally I asked him if he really heard horses walking on cobblestones, wouldn't there be some kind of stones out there instead of just grass? I tried to pacify him by saying he'd probably just heard Busch's Clydesdales walking around down on

Pestalozzi Street, a couple of blocks away. But he really got mad then, and insisted he heard the horses in a stone courtyard right underneath his window every night.

"Later that summer, we looked out the window and saw the grass was drying up on little squares. We dug it up, and found a tile courtyard about six inches below the topsoil. The tiles all dated from 1878. They were so beautiful we decided to tile the basement floor with them. We needed 1167 tiles, and found 1150. We also found out that they were part of an old stone courtyard where the 'Lavender Lady's' carriage was brought out to be hitched up to her horses. A few weeks after that, the painter returned to California. He was convinced that he had been vindicated, even though nobody else had ever heard the phantom horses. "When we were still restoring the place, my son came down as a night watchman. He brought along his pet Doberman Pinscher who we called Shadow because she would never leave him. But when they got here, he couldn't get the dog to go in the house. Even when he used a choke chain, she wouldn't move. She'd whine, lie down, and even try to bite him. I told him to put her underneath the back entranceway because she'd be satisfied there, and stay put. But then the dog just disappeared. We figured she was either stolen, or just ran away.

"Three years later, after the restaurant opened, a lady called my son over to her table. He was waiting the downstairs dining room, and she thought he was just another waiter. She said she'd been one of the servants who discovered the last Lemp suicide, and wanted to tell somebody at the restaurant about what happened. She told him that about nine o'clock in the morning, she and her husband used to bring Charles his breakfast. But that morning, they heard a sound like a firecracker. About five minutes later, they heard another pop. She said to her husband that something must have happened, and he'd better go check. They lived in the old carriage house and Charles had the back downstairs room in the main house. Her husband went through the back downstairs entranceway, but quickly came back. He told her something strange had happened. Charles had killed himself and his dog. The dog was shot once through the heart, and he'd shot himself through the head.

"Then my son told her he knew what kind of dog Charles had. 'It was a Doberman Pinscher.' She was really surprised that he was right, and asked him how he knew. He just shrugged his shoulders, though, and didn't explain, but he stared a long time at the nearby back door his own Doberman Pinscher had refused to enter.

"A lot of this is irony, but you piece it all together and pretty soon you have a lot of information that is very impressive."

Dick explained what he meant. "We have a woman who comes here quite often to take snapshots, and on each picture, a monkey face shows up. When we were first repairing the house, two elderly ladies stopped by who had gone to grade school in the neighborhood. They asked us where the Lemps kept the monkey boy. I didn't know what they were talking about, so I asked them what they meant. They said that, as children, they walked to school every day past the Lemp house, and they were always frightened by a face in an upstairs window that looked like a monkey-boy. Well, it turned out that the family records didn't agree on the number of Lemp children. There was always conflicting numbers, and now some people claim that a deformed child was kept home in the attic. Anyway, the face that the two elderly women described is the same face that keeps turning up in all the photographs taken at the house.

"Maybe it's all hearsay, but there are strange things that happen here. My nephew whom I hadn't seen for twenty years visited from Seattle. He called to say he was coming through town, had seen the house on national television, and asked if he could visit it. We came on Saturday morning and went into the bar. Friday night, I'd cleaned the place up myself. But when we went downstairs, I noticed a burgundy glass on the bar that hadn't been there before. I remember thinking, 'How the hell did that get there?' Just then, my nephew said he didn't believe the house was haunted, and told me I probably made all the stories up. That's when the burgundy glass jumped about a foot and a half off the bar and shattered on the floor about fifty feet away! My nephew said it was a trick, but I just laughed because those kinds of things happen quite a bit. They happen, but there's no logical explanation.

"One time, I even heard a voice say, 'Hi Mom, Hi Mom!' as my wife entered a room. She asked me if I'd said something, but I hadn't. And I know she didn't say anything because I was watching her. We called a waiter over. He'd heard it, too. None of us had said a thing. But someone had.

"Another night, my son was tending bar with a waiter when the piano keys started playing by themselves. The piano was over thirty feet from anybody who could play it, and the piano lid was shut tight! That scared them both.

"Psychics from as far away as Los Angeles and New York have visited, and left convinced this place is haunted. Most of them identify the ghost as Charles, and confirm that he killed himself with a gun. A few years back, a reporter for the *St. Louis Post-Dispatch* and a famous psychic visited haunted houses all over the St. Louis area. Nothing happened at any of them. But when they were getting ready to leave here, every table in the dining room started shaking."

Dick Pointer laughed when he told the story. "Is it haunted? My wife thinks there are friendly spirits here that just don't want to leave their old home. My son thinks the place isn't haunted. But I'm convinced that it is. And I believe that if anybody wants to come, and stay a reasonable amount of time here, they'll find out. Something out of the ordinary will happen. I'd bet on it." Dick Pointer laughed again.

He obviously thoroughly enjoyed owning the place. And even if there was a restless spirit or two there, at least its present owner has found peace in the Lemp House.

THE SPIRITS OF ST. LOUIS

The old Alexian Brothers Hospital,
site of *"the real St. Louis Exorcist Case."*

(photo courtesy of the
Missouri Historical Society)

*S*t. Louis ghost stories have been around almost as long as St. Louis—at least, according to old newspapers I'd found in libraries around town. Over a century ago, local hauntings were regularly reported along with all the other gossip and news about the city. But that didn't mean belief in ghosts was accepted by everybody. One article, from 1853, told of a prominent St. Louis businessman who was kicked out of his church for believing in ghosts. At his trial for "heresy," Henry Stagg made a spirited defense.

"It is now an established fact, beyond the shadow of a doubt in the minds of hundreds and thousands of our best citizens, that Spirits—our departed brothers and sisters, parents, children and friends—do really hold converse with them, assuring them that they are not dead, but alive, and imparting to them consoling thoughts of their happy and glorified condition. And notwithstanding the bitter and malevolent opposition with which this startling phenomenon has been met by churches, and religious and secular press during the last five years, it has steadily advanced, step by step, spreading in every direction throughout the length and breadth of the land, and extending into different parts of Europe, converting its thousands, including some of the ablest minds of the day, until at length the Clergy, completely outdone, have been compelled to acknowledge the truth, that Spirits do communicate."

A lot of people agreed with Henry Stagg. But not the Second Baptist Church. They asked him to take his beliefs elsewhere. Of course, that was years before the present congregation moved out to Clayton Road and experienced the supernatural first hand in their own Church House.

Dr. Joseph Nash McDowell. *"...and I distinctly saw my dear, dead mother, standing a little distance off, beckoning me."*

(photo courtesy of the Missouri Historical Society)

I never found out why Henry Stagg believed in ghosts so strongly, but I did come across a story that helped convince one of his skeptical contemporaries to believe in the supernatural.

Before the Civil War, Dr. Joseph Nash McDowell was St. Louis' leading surgeon. He was the founder of the first successful medical school west of the Mississippi. And he was also an outspoken critic of anyone who believed in ghosts or other "such frauds without foundation." But that was before he claimed his dead mother's spirit saved his life. Shortly before his own death in 1861, he commented on his change of heart.

"A German girl died with a very unusual disease, and we were determined to get her body for dissection. We got it and laid it in the college. The secret leaked out, and the Germans got their backs up and made things lively for us. It was planned by them to come one night and hunt over the college to see if the body was there to be dissected.

"I received a note at my house at nine o'clock in the evening, warning me that the visit was to be that night. I went down to the college about eleven o'clock thinking to hide the corpse. When I got there, all was quiet. I went through the dissecting room, with a small lantern in my hand, in the direction of the body. I picked the cadaver up, and threw it over my shoulder to carry it to the top loft to conceal it between the rafters, or place it in a cedar chest that had stood in a closet for years.

"I had ascended one flight of stairs, when out went my lamp. I laid down the corpse, and restruck a light. I then picked up the body, when out went my light again. I felt for another match in my pocket, when I distinctly saw my dear, dead mother, standing a little distance off, beckoning to me.

"In the middle of the passage was a window; I saw her rise in front of it. I walked along close to the wall, with the corpse over my shoulder, and went to the top loft and hid it. I came down in the dark, for I knew the way well. As I reached the window in the passage, there were two Germans talking. One had a shotgun, the other a revolver. I kept close to the wall, and slid down the stairs. When I got to the dissecting room door, I looked down the stairs into the hallway. There I saw five or six men lighting a lamp. I hesitated a moment as to what I should do, as I had left my pistols in my pocket in the dissecting room where I took the body. I looked in the room, as it was my only chance to get away, when I saw my spirit mother standing near the table from which I had taken the corpse. I had no light, but the halo that surrounded my mother was sufficient to enable me to see the table quite plainly.

"I heard the men coming up the stairs. I laid down whence I had taken the body, and pulled a cloth over my face to hide it. The men came in, all of them being armed, to look at the dead. They uncovered one body—it was that of a man, the next a man; then they came to two women with black hair—the girl they were looking for had light flaxen hair. Then they passed me; one German said; 'Here is a fellow who died in his boots; I guess he's a fresh one.'

"I laid like marble. I thought I would jump up and frighten them. But I heard a voice, soft and low, close to my ear, say, 'Be still, be still.' The men went over the building and finally down the stairs. I waited awhile, then slipped out. At the corner of Gratiot Street, I heard three men talking German. But they took no notice of me, and I went safely home."

Dr. McDowell and Henry Stagg seemed to be in good company. The old newspapers reported dozens of supernatural tales. Over the years, St. Louisans in the last century reported seeing a ghost at the old Fourth District Police Station at Twelfth and Monroe, and Kate Black's luminescent spirit at her haunted rooming house

DR. McDOWELL'S OLD MEDICAL COLLEGE

Dr. McDowell's Medical College
(photo courtesy of the Missouri Historical Society)

between Sixth and Poplar Streets. And the disembodied ghoul in downtown's famous Southern Hotel was almost as well-known a local landmark as the hotel itself.

In 1915, front pages even bannered the literary appearance of a "real St. Louis ghost writer." For the next 25 years, Patience Worth, the spirit of a long dead sixteenth-century spinster, supposedly dictated full-length novels and thousands of poems through a Ouija board to a St. Louis housewife. Writings that were eventually read and praised around the world originated from a parlor game in a middle-class house on Kingsbury Boulevard.

More recent articles told of the haunted Cupples Mansion on the campus of St. Louis University and of Powell Symphony Hall's resident ghost. But in 1949, St. Louis' supernatural horror stories reached a chilling climax.

I'd always heard there was a St. Louis connection to the book and film, *The Exorcist*. But details were hard to come by. News stories from the time made only vague references. And the old clippings file at the St. Louis Public Library was, for once, empty. Then the librarian gave me the name of a woman from another department who might be able to help. After a long search, I found her in a lonely, isolated wing of the library. When I explained what I was looking for, she stared right through me for a long time without saying a word. She seemed to be deciding whether or not to trust me.

Finally, she excused herself, and returned from another room with a folder crammed with clippings, notes, and articles on the real "St. Louis Exorcist Case." She explained they were her personal files. They did not belong to the library. And she wanted them all returned. For reasons she wouldn't go into, she'd followed and collected every shred of news about the incident for over thirty years.

The story, in bits and pieces, was all there. It had begun near Washington, D.C., with scratching in the walls. A fourteen-year-old boy was the main character. He'd been introduced to the supernatural by his late St. Louis aunt, through the Ouija board. Shortly after her death, the scratching sounds became footsteps that centered in his room. From that beginning, he gradually changed and became transformed into the powerfully grotesque creature that convinced the Catholic Church hierarchy to allow the first authorized exorcism in America in over 100 years.

Strange writings on his back, chest and thighs spelled out LOUIS, convincing his family that the exorcism was meant to take place in St. Louis. At first, he stayed at the old family home in Webster Groves. Later, he was moved to DuBourg Hall on the St. Louis University campus. But after his violent reactions to the exorcism ritual, he was again moved, this time to the Alexian Brothers Hospital in South St. Louis. The nightmare continued for four long months until, finally, the struggle ended, almost as dramatically and suddenly as it began. The "demon" was expelled. The boy remembered nothing. And the exorcist returned to his priestly duties. For the rest of his life, he never again discussed the case.

The librarian gave me names and telephone numbers of people associated with the events of 30 years ago. Many of them still seemed afraid and bothered by their memories. Years had passed, but not their fears. But they reluctantly talked and even shared other names with me.

A former security guard and several others at St. Louis University told of the exorcist losing over 60 pounds during the ordeal, almost as much as the boy weighed. A nurse at the hospital told stories of the small child's unnatural strength, of levitations and smashed furniture, and the "dropping, freezing temperatures in his room." And an older priest, who had been a seminarian-attendant at the hospital during the nightly rituals, firmly stated, "There was no denying it. If you had seen it, you would know it was all true. There is a Devil—believe in it. If nothing else, believe in it. It is the one thing worth fearing."

The exorcist himself remained silent. In 1983, he died in St. Louis on the 34th anniversary of the exorcism.

The old Alexian Brothers Hospital is gone, too. A worker at the new hospital explained that "The room where it all happened was locked up and never used again. We couldn't get the lights to stay on, or keep heat in there. It was always freezing cold. Later, the rooms on either side were closed too. Then the entire floor was shut off. We used it for storage for a while, but most of the hospital staff were afraid to go up there. In 1978, the old building was torn down, but not without problems. The demolition crew couldn't control the headache ball when that floor was being taken off. The ball swung around and hit the new building. But it finally was destroyed, and we were very glad and relieved to see it gone."

Not all of St. Louis' tales of the supernatural are as serious or dark as the exorcist's story. In north St. Louis, close to my own boyhood home, sits the historic Hyde Park Bissell Mansion, now a restaurant. Ever since I could remember, I'd heard stories that the beautiful house overlooking the Mississippi River was home to one or more friendly ghosts. After the heaviness of the exorcism story, I needed a friendly ghost story. So I followed the river north to check it out.

The house was built in 1823, the first brick home in St. Louis. At one time, it was the center of a nearly 2000-acre farm. But, today, it's hemmed in on all sides by the apartments and homes of the city. Since it's now a restaurant, I visited between the lunch and dinner

Becky Schepker.
"We called the ghost Captain Bissell and would walk through the
empty house calling, 'Oh Captain Bissell, bring our cat back!' "

hours. Its manager was Becky Schepker, an attractive young woman, who'd grown up in the neighborhood. In fact, she'd often played in the house as a child.

"This is the nosiest house on earth," she said. "It never scares me, though. But, sometimes, it gets so loud that I just decide to leave for a while. When I was little and spent a lot of time here, we always believed it was haunted. There was a ceramic cat that sat on the window ledge at the top of the landing. It used to disappear periodically. To us, it was just another game. We called the ghost Captain Bissell and would walk through the empty house calling, 'Oh Captain Bissell, bring our cat back!' We'd go through the whole house, calling for him to bring it back. Then, by the time we'd get back to the landing, we'd find it sitting there again!

"The last lady who lived in the house really believed in spirits. She claimed she was constantly in touch with them, most of which were children. In fact, around holidays, especially Christmas Eve, lots of people claim they can hear the children's spirits laughing, running and playing in the empty rooms. Sometimes their excited sounds are so loud that it's hard to carry on a normal conversation!

"Psychics who've visited say there are lots of ghosts in the mansion and that they are all good. They've also said there is a spirit of a man who is outside, and never comes in. But he's also a good spirit, and seems to protect the place.

"Sometimes when the sounds start," Becky went on, "I've gone looking for them myself, but I've never seen anything. They seem to especially emanate from the upstairs north bedroom. And, every once in a while, when I'd go upstairs searching, I'd climb the back stairs and return down the front. On those times, I would imagine— even sort of hear—the sound of music in the downstairs hall. And I'd picture that, when I turned the corner, I'd see the hall full of people dressed up in old-fashioned party clothes for a special occasion years ago. I figured it was just my imagination.

"But one time, a local writer came here on tour with a group of people. When she was upstairs, I overheard her read the exact account of the scene, just as I'd always imagined. I asked where she had gotten the description. And she said it was an actual eyewitness account of the wedding of Captain Bissell's daughter. She'd dressed in her old bedroom on the north side of the house, come down the steps on her father's arm, turned on the landing, come down the front hall with the music playing. The account was exactly as I'd so often visualized it. And to this day, I still wonder how I knew an image so well that I'd never read or seen or experienced at all during my own lifetime."

Childhood spirits must like north St. Louis. If the Bissell Mansion's ghosts conjure up the playful noise and happy images of a child's memories, then Walnut Park's haunted house on Garesche is a home to the inquisitive spirits of curious infants.

Lisa Scales of University City told the story of her aunt's home, which is just a few minutes' drive from the Bissell Mansion.

"After my grandmother bought the house, she and my aunts would wake up at night and hear footsteps coming up the stairs. And during the day, they'd hear them downstairs, too. Then, when my Aunt Joyce's son, Peter, was still a little boy, he became frightened because he said 'babies' were watching him. Well, there weren't any other babies in the house, so we just thought he was imagining things.

Lisa Scales. *"...then whatever it was sat on the edge of her bed."*

"One night, my Aunt Cheryl was home alone with Peter. He was asleep upstairs when she heard a baby crying. She went up to check on Peter, but he was sound asleep. When she got back downstairs, she could still hear a crying baby. So she went upstairs again, and found Peter asleep. Then she brought him downstairs to the living room. But from the empty second floor she could still clearly hear the crying sounds of a baby who wasn't there. Later, Aunt Cheryl woke up one night and saw two little babies on the edge of the bed watching her. They looked like any other two infants, except they were blue. And when she looked again, they were gone.

"When my Aunt Marlene was growing up in the house, she was always afraid to go upstairs by herself. She swore little babies would be peeking around the corners at her.

"Later, they had problems with other ghosts, too. One night, when my Aunt Rita was asleep upstairs, she woke up and felt that someone else was in the room with her. She thought it was another of my aunts, so she didn't turn over. Then, whatever it was, sat on the edge of her bed. But she still didn't look to see who it was.

"That's when it laid on top of her! She couldn't move. She couldn't even breathe. After about a minute, it slowly got up. She turned her head, looked and saw the outline of a man. He was about six feet tall and walked into the closet at the foot of the bed! She screamed, and woke everybody up. It was a week before she slept in that bed again.

"Another one of my aunts came home one night, went upstairs, and saw the same faint outline of a man sitting on the bed. He was just looking out the window. As she got to the top of the steps, he disappeared into the closet, too!

"Nowadays, they just take that haunted stuff in stride. I guess they're used to the ghosts. Sometimes, they still get scared. But they don't do anything about it since the ghosts have never hurt them. And they've never bothered the ghosts. They just leave each other alone. And that seems to suit everybody in the house just fine!"

Not everybody adjusts so easily to sharing their house with a ghost. About halfway between the house on Garesche and the Bissell Mansion on Randall is a large brick home on Fair Avenue. It once belonged to Elizabeth Hernandez's family. When they came to believe the place was haunted, though, they decided it was time to move on.

I'd known Liz for years. But it was only when I began researching this book that she explained why her family had decided to move from her beautiful childhood home.

"My mother, and her mother before her, always had the ability to foretell the future. But when we moved into our house on Fair, we didn't know we'd eventually move out, believing the place was haunted by a ghost. We lived there a long time before anything happened. But, in the summer of 1966, my cousins came to visit us. Late one

Liz Hernandez Sanders. *"It was as if, when we tried to ignore it, the sound would get louder and more persistent."*

night, about twelve-thirty, we were just settling down to go to sleep when I heard what sounded like rattling chains. My cousin heard it also but, when we listened at the windows, we couldn't hear anything outside. After a while it stopped, so we lay back down. But a few minutes later, we heard it again. It was as if, when we tried to ignore it, the sound would get louder and more persistent.

"I couldn't figure it out. I thought it might be prowlers, so my cousin and I both got up and searched the entire house. We didn't find anything unusual, but we could still hear the chains rattling. When we went back to bed, we couldn't sleep, though, because of the noise. But now it sounded like it was in the house! Then I thought I'd figured it out. I imagined our dog, Cleo, had gone to sleep with her walking chain on. I accidently woke my mother up looking for the dog. Of course, she wanted to know what I was doing. So I explained I kept hearing chains, and thought it was Cleo. Then I asked if she'd been praying her rosary. She said that even if she had, we'd never have heard it in the other room. And the dog was with her, but without its chain! With that, she told us to stop being silly, and go back to sleep!

"We agreed, went back to bed, and the rattling chains started again. We quietly got up, and made our way through the dark house searching for the sounds. When we got even with the butler's pantry, which was directly over the basement stairwell, I could clearly hear them. They were so loud, I said to my cousin, 'Oh, my God, they're in the basement!' We ran over to the door and locked it. Then we felt a little relieved with that heavy door safely bolted, so no one could get upstairs. And there was nothing of value in the basement. I was so tired. All I could think was that whoever it was would get tired, too and leave!

"We tried to go to sleep, but the chains became even louder. I woke my mother again, but she insisted it was just my imagination. By that time, I half-believed her. Neither my cousin nor I could fall asleep, though. So we got another cousin up to play cards. At least we wouldn't be alone. She really teased us about it, but finally settled down to the game. Then the rattling became louder. By that time, I refused to pay any attention to it, but my cousin's eyes got bigger and bigger. She asked if we heard the chains. But we wouldn't admit it. They got louder, and louder, and louder. The more we ignored it, the louder they got. My cousin finally cried, 'Okay, okay, I believe you. I hear the chains!'

"With that, I got my cousin, Johnny, up. We were convinced there had, to be somebody in the house. We searched every room, and even the attic. We were just too frightened to go to sleep. We checked everywhere but the basement. We knew somebody was down there! But the door was safely locked. The rest of the house was safe.

"It was now nearly three a.m. and we were all exhausted. To everyone's relief, the sounds of the rattling chains abruptly stopped. So we returned to bed. But just as we started to doze off, we heard footsteps in the attic. It was like somebody was pacing back and forth, directly over us. The pacing stopped right at the door which led down the stairway to my room.

"I kept lying there wondering whether I was imagining the new sounds. Then my cousin, who was sharing my room, asked if I heard footsteps in the attic. I was almost too frightened to answer, because the door up there did not lock. And it was the only thing keeping whatever was upstairs away from my room.

"We finally got the courage to make our way to Johnny's room. But he didn't believe us, because he'd already searched the attic. We begged him to check it again. Grumpily, he agreed. The three of us made our way to the top of the stairs with a flashlight. We opened the door and snatched on the light. We searched the entire attic. There was nobody there. And there was no place to hide. We felt better. We turned off the light, shut the door, and went down the stairs.

"My mother was waiting for us. She was furious with us for letting our imaginations get the best of us. We quickly went to bed. But as soon as we lay down, the pacing in the attic started again. Back and forth, back and forth. And then it would stop at the door at the top of the stairs. The only safety we had was the attic door that had no lock! We very quietly moved into my mother's room, firmly pressed our feet against her closed door, and fell into an exhausted sleep.

"About five-thirty, my mother got up and went into the kitchen to fix some coffee. But as soon as she sat down, she heard a terrible moaning, as if someone were in great pain. She quickly rushed to my uncle's bedroom door. He'd been very sick, and she was afraid he was ill. But when she opened the door, my uncle was sitting up in bed. He'd heard the terrible moaning, too. Just then, they heard it again. It was coming from the basement. It was the most pitiful sound they'd ever heard, as if someone were in severe physical pain. My mother rushed right in to tell us there really was somebody in the house. But, by that time, I was too tired to care.

"Finally, the sounds stopped. When I got up to go to work, I made everyone promise not go down in the basement unless the police were called. But, after I left, they took the key, unlocked the door, and searched the basement. All the doors down there were locked from the inside. The windows were, too. And they were also guarded by heavy bars. No one could have gotten in, or out, without leaving a door or window unlocked. And there was nothing disturbed.

"It wasn't until I got home, that I thought maybe 'it' wasn't human. We'd never had any problems before with rattling chains or pacing footsteps. But that night was only the beginning.

"I began waking up with the same recurring nightmare. There would be a person standing over me—a man. He kept shaking me and telling me to wake up. After that, I always woke with a start. It was as if someone had pushed me awake. Shortly after all these things had begun, my brother came to stay with us. He stayed in the same room where I first heard the strange sounds. He was almost asleep one night, when he saw me going down the hall to my mother's room. He called but I didn't answer. So he became worried because that wasn't like me. He got up and followed me into the room, calling my name. But when he got there, my mother told him that no one was there but her. He insisted he'd followed me—but I wasn't there. I was sound asleep in my own bed.

"A short time after we began experiencing things, we talked with our neighbors about the problems. They told us the house's previous owner had been ill with a terminal disease. He'd become so depressed that he tried to hang himself in the basement. His daughter found him when she came home and rushed him to the hospital. But he died there. When he was alive, though, his favorite room had been the attic. It had been built especially for him. It was his favorite place. And he seldom left it.

"Within a year, we sold the house and moved. Just too many things had happened. And we never really felt safe, or completely at rest, in that house again."

After listening to Liz's story, I decided to drive down to the old neighborhood where we'd both grown up. The hallway where I'd met my only ghost was still there. And so was Liz's big house on Fair Avenue. A few blocks away, I stopped at the Bellefontaine and Calvary Cemeteries. When we were kids, we'd always heard that a ghostly hitchhiker haunted the road between these two oldest graveyards in

North St. Louis. But I'd never met anybody who'd actually seen the ghost. And this time was no different.

What I did find in the cemeteries though, were lots of familiar names. Henry Stagg is buried there, and so is Dr. McDowell. Kate Black's landlady, Patience Worth's 'editor', and the Southern Hotel's ghostly guest are all interred there, too. Fine family plots represent the proud Bissell and Clemens family names, but the Exorcist is found in a very simple priestly grave. High on a hilltop, overlooking the Mississippi River, is the Cupples tomb. And across the road is the large Lemp family mausoleum. Only 12 of its 32 crypts have been used. The others wait empty, for a family that is no more.

On the many tombstones are epitaphs that reminded me of cemeteries I'd visited up and down the river. From Hannibal in the north, to Cape Girardeau in the south, the memories of dozens of stories and storytellers rushed through my mind. And, after all the miles and all the tales of ghostly hauntings, I still found myself wondering. Was the most hopeful epitaph also a question...

REST IN PEACE (?)

The Cupples tomb in Bellefontaine Cemetery.

EPILOGUE

View down river from the old
Kaskaskia Cemetery.
*"Ending my haunted odyssey was proving
to be a lot harder than I thought."*

My haunted odyssey was drawing to a close. It had begun when I was a small boy, and for four years had taken me into homes and towns and cities up and down the Mississippi Valley. One more time, I retraced my travels and revisited many of the friends I'd met along the way.

The folks in Ste. Genevieve were busily preparing for their city's 250th birthday, but they mentioned that, when things settled down again, some local families had some stories they wanted to share with me. Across the river, Norman Picou had recently retired from Kaskaskia's only school, and he and Naomi were reading, painting, and generally enjoying life on Kaskaskia's doomed island.

Mike Garrity had graduated from the university. His old fraternity house was now used as the school's infirmary. Mike explained, "The frat just couldn't get members to stay in the house anymore." Ann Abbott proudly showed off the new home of the local theater company. She reluctantly admitted, though, that the ghost at the Cape River Heritage Museum hadn't moved with them.

Doug and Bev Elliot reported just the opposite. They're renovating another large historic house near Edwardsville, and, over breakfast they shared with me recently, they told of the terrible night they were awakened by a phone call. They rushed over to watch the Three Mile House burn. Bev sadly described the heartbreaking experience and Doug added, "I couldn't help myself I walked up and asked all the spirits that were still earthbound to come home with us. I have to admit, too—things have been a lot louder at home since that night."

Everything is quiet, though, with St. Charles' Henry Evans. He was enjoying retirement and even used my visit to introduce a former student who had some recent supernatural experiences to discuss.

Out in Augusta, its resident blacksmith claimed, "Things are just about the same. The ghost has his good days and bad, and sometimes he still gets angry with me. But last summer, early one morning, I glanced up and, for the first time, I actually saw him. He was just standing in the doorway, staring at me with the most piercing eyes I've ever seen in my life. He was dressed just like an old time French frontiersman. But when I looked up again, he was gone."

Lincoln County's Ezra Tillotson had grown a full beard. Otherwise, he's still the same—still teaching every day and keeping the clock for Clopton High School's champion basketball teams. Moabious Gentry and his wife are happily living in their modern, solar-heated hillside home, and down the road, Mattie Rose Wallace is in her farmhouse, lovingly surrounded by her children, grandchildren, and great-grandchildren. The spirits of Lincoln County all seemed to be as content as their storytellers.

The lonely phantoms of Pike County haven't shown themselves much, either. In fact, up in Louisiana, Ray and Pat Duckworth recently sold their "haunted house" to a new radio station. They heartily approve of the music being played and, apparently, so does its resident ghost, because they haven't heard of her locking any of the radio personnel in, or out of, the station. Although they did mention a neighbor who seemed to be having a problem with "a particularly cantankerous ghost."

Up in Hannibal, Judge Ogle was still traveling between Marion County's two court houses. But he hadn't seen any ghostly carriages passing him on the road lately. And Carolyn Williams and her mother were almost as proud of their beautiful Stonecraft Manor being listed on the National Register of Historic Places, as they were relieved that they hadn't been troubled by any "new disturbances." On the other hand, Mary Wamsley greeted me with, "I hoped after your last visit that things might have settled down when we talked it all out. But this house is worse haunted than ever."

Back in St. Louis, the ghosts and their activities remain as diverse as their storytellers. Dick Pointer related that the Lemp

House hauntings were "active as usual." And at the Bissell and Myer houses, ghostly tales of the gentler variety continue to be reported. The Fathmans volunteered that everything was quiet at their home in University City, as did the Sears family in Kirkwood and Cathy Mueller in Webster Groves.

But new stories, and storytellers, continue to pop up. And even the older storytellers sometimes have new yarns to spin. To celebrate, belatedly, his cousin Sam's 150th birthday, and, as well, the close of my haunted odyssey, I took Mr. Cyril Clemens to lunch. We drove down to Crown's Candy Kitchen, the oldest ice cream parlor in St. Louis, which is just a few blocks from the childhood homes of both Mr. Clemens' grandfather and my own.

Since it had been years since Mr. Clemens had been back in the old neighborhood, we visited the house his grandfather had built back in the 1840s. The old mansion was constructed as a living memorial to his dead wife, and her death mask in cast iron can still be seen above every window. The visit triggered an outpouring of Clemens' family superstitions and half-forgotten ghost stories.

Ending my haunted odyssey was proving to be a lot harder that I had thought. Mr. Clemens' new tales whetted my appetite for more. And Doug and Bev Elliot have invited me to visit their renovated house and investigate their new ghost stories for myself. The Duckworths had given me the name and telephone number of their neighbor with "the cantankerous ghost." And Augusta's blacksmith has friends with a haunted house up in Galena, Illinois. Then there were still the names of folks I'd never had time to visit in Ste. Genevieve, Belleville, New Madrid, and Keokuk. Not to mention the fact that I haven't yet met my "second ghost"! Maybe this coming weekend, I could do a little traveling.

Anybody know a good long dark hallway where I should look?

ABOUT THE AUTHOR

James McMurtry Longo is a master storyteller, whether showcasing his talents at the International Storytelling Festival beneath the Gateway Arch in his hometown of St. Louis, at the schools and universities on three continents where he has taught, around the campfires of the summer camps he has directed, or in the eight books he has written.

Jim began his writing career as the sports editor of his school newspaper. Today, he is chair of the Education Department at Washington & Jefferson College. His latest book, *From Classroom to White House: Presidents and First Ladies as Students and Teachers*, published by McFarland in 2011, won rave reviews from coast to coast.

His trilogy of ghost story collections—*Haunted Odyssey, Ghosts Along the Mississippi* and *Favorite Haunts*—solidified his national reputation as a "storyteller extraordinaire," as heralded by WPST Philadelphia.

Jim's 2008 book, *Isabel Orleans-Bragança: The Brazilian Princess Who Freed the Slaves*, published by McFarland, was nominated for Yale University's Frederick Douglass Book Prize as the "most outstanding non-fiction book in English on the subject of slavery and abolition." It was also nominated for the Robert F. Kennedy Center for Justice and Human Rights Book Award.

When Jim was serving as the Fulbright Distinguished Chair of the Gender and Women's Study Program at

Austria's Alpen-Adria University of Klagenfurt, that biography caught the attention of the great-granddaughter of Archduke Franz Ferdinand, whose assassination sparked World War I. The mysterious circumstances of that murder and its connections to Adolf Hitler is the focus of Jim's forthcoming book *VENDETTA: Hitler's War Against a Vanished Empire, a Dead Archduke, and his Royal Orphans.*

His research and teaching have taken him to Austria, Brazil, Costa Rica, Portugal, England, Scotland, Wales, Germany, the Czech Republic, and Canada. He holds an Ed.D. in Teaching, Curriculum, and Learning from Harvard University, an M.A.T. in Curriculum Writing and Design from Webster University, and a B.S. in Education and History from University of Missouri—St. Louis.

Jim believes all he ever needed to know he learned at summer camp. When not teaching or writing, he would rather be in a canoe than any other place on earth. He lives in Washington, Pa., with his wife.

Thanks for reading this Factual Planet Chronicle.

Knowledge unshared is knowledge lost, so if you loved

this book, be sure to share it with your friends and

followers or post a short review with your favorite

bookseller or forum!